A RIOT
OF WRITERS

A Romp Through English Literature

TERRANCE DICKS
Illustrated by RAY JELLIFFE

Piccadilly Press · London

Phototypeset by Goodfellow & Egan, Cambridge
Printed and bound by Hartnolls Ltd., Bodmin, Cornwall
for the publishers, Piccadilly Press Ltd.,
5 Castle Road, London NW1 8PR

A catalogue record for this book is available
from the British Library

ISBN: 1–85340–128–5 (trade paperback)
ISBN: 1–85340–142–0 (hardback)

Terrance Dicks is British and lives in North London with his wife and three
sons. A very well-known author, he has written over a hundred books for
children including the following series for Piccadilly Press: *The Adventures
of David & Goliath, Jonathan's Ghost, A Cat Called Max* and *The MacMagics*.
Piccadilly Press has also recently published his popular *Europe United*.

Ray Jelliffe is British and lives in Berkshire with his wife. Now retired, but
working harder than ever, he used to be a creative director of a large
advertising agency. He has illustrated numerous greetings cards and
several books, including *Europe United*.

Contents

Introduction

Scribble, Scribble, Scribble . . .

'Another damned thick, square book! Always scribble, scribble, scribble. Eh! Mr Gibbon?'

– The Duke of Gloucester, on being presented, by the proud writer, with the latest volume of Mr Gibbon's massive, many-volumed 'Decline and Fall of the Roman Empire'.

Let's face it – it's all too easy to sympathise with the Duke. There's a lot of Eng Lit. Long before Gibbon, and long after, writers have been scribbling away, producing many a damned thick book, and slim, sensitive volume. 'Of making many books there is no end . . .' Don't let it worry you.

Writers deal with the basics – and they don't change much. Get past the odd bit of funny spelling and old-fashioned expression and you're into sex, love, hate, power, money, ambition . . .

'Bred any good rooks lately?'

The themes of Shakespeare and Dickens are the same as those of 'Dynasty' and 'Dallas'.

This book will give you a (very) rough guide to the wonderful world of Eng Lit. Since there are so many great writers to choose from, we've been forced to go for just the very top names, the real classics. Even so, quite a few worthy writers have had to be left out. It's hard to say exactly what makes a classic writer. A good rule of thumb is, have they stood the test of time? So we've drawn a line at the end of the nineteenth century – everybody in this book was born before 1900 . . .

Chapter One

GEOFFREY CHAUCER
1340–1400

Opening for England

The first major writer to work in (more or less) recognisable English was a fourteenth century yuppie called Geoffrey Chaucer. Son of a wine-merchant, young Geoffrey got a post, probably through Dad's influence, as page in one of the royal households.

'Dad's got me a job as a page – one day I might be a book!'

I Spy Chaucer

A few years later he was a soldier in France, where he was captured but later ransomed. He studied at the Inner Temple in London for a while, and became a diplomat. By 1366 he was travelling to Spain on a Government mission. He was to make many more such trips abroad 'on the King's business' and it seems more than likely he was a secret agent. (You can imagine our boy in some Spanish tavern, ordering a pot of mulled wine, shaken but not stirred, eyeing some spicy señorita and murmuring 'The name's Chaucer – Geoffrey Chaucer . . .')

Chaucer's Career

Home from his travels, he settled down, married his childhood sweetheart, and became a top civil servant.

Despite his busy career, he found time for writing. He began with such poems as 'The Book of the Duchess', 'The House of Fame',

'The Parliament of Fowls', 'Troilus and Criseyde' and many more. Chaucer's masterpiece, however, is a long narrative poem, 'The Canterbury Tales'.

The Pilgrim Package

In those days people went on pilgrimage to Canterbury, to visit the tomb of the martyred archbishop, Thomas à Becket. It was a sort of spiritual package tour, combining a bit of a jaunt with a chance to clock up a few points in heaven. And as Chaucer pointed out, as soon as spring was here:

'Thanne longen folke to goon on pilgrimage'.

Chaucer gives us, in the poem's Prologue, thumbnail sketches of a typical batch of pilgrims. He starts with a noble Knight, assuring us:

'He was a verray parfit, gentil Knight'.

A Mixed Bag

Almost too good to be true, in fact. But don't worry, the other travellers are more human and believable. The apparently-saintly Prioress has more than her share of worldly vanity and pretension:

'Ful weel she soong the servyce dyvyne
Entuned in hir nose ful semely
And Frenssh she spak ful fair and fetisely
After the scole of Stratford atte Bowe
For Frenssh of Parys was to hire unknowe . . .'

The fat Monk is far too fond of food and drink and hunting:

'He was not pale as a forpyned goost', Chaucer tells us.

'I only go for the Canterbury lamb and mint sauce!'

There's a Merchant, not above cutting a few corners, and not so financially sound as he'd like his fellow businessmen to think:

'There wiste no wight that he was in dette . . .'

The Sergeant of Law does well out of dodgy land deals. The Miller is a brawny, boozy thug who cheats his customers. The Wife of Bath, an early feminist, is a tough cookie. An expert on marriage, she's worn out five husbands already:

'She was a worthy womman al hir lyve
Housebondes at chirche dore she hadde fyve.'

Some Dodgy Deals

The charming friar is an expert at conning cash out of wealthy widows.

The Summoner, an important church official is a pimply-faced horror, a dedicated boozer and a lecherous corrupter of the young. His mate, the Pardoner, is a sinister-looking type who sells fake holy relics to the poor.

Telling the Tale

The pilgrims take turns telling stories. The Knight tells a touching tale of love and chivalry. The Miller, who's next, comes up with an X-certificate tale about an old carpenter, his beautiful young wife and their lusty lodger. The climax involves a bare bottom stuck out

of the window and someone waiting with a hot iron . . . I've always admired the final couplet:

> 'Now Nicholas is branded on the bum
> So ends my tale; God bless us every one!'

(The other dirty story, the Summoner's, has Eng Lit's first fart joke.)

The Church Under Attack
There are twenty-three tales in all, but the best part of 'The Canterbury Tales' is undoubtedly the Prologue itself. It gives us a splendidly assorted group of characters, a vivid picture of four-teenth century life and a devastatingly frank criticism of a powerful, often-corrupt Church.

(This was quite a brave thing to do at the time – many a writer has – literally – lost his head for being satirical about the wrong people.)

First Man In
Chaucer has an excellent claim to be the founder of Eng Lit, and he deserves his place as the original inhabitant of Westminster Abbey's Poets' Corner.

Chaucer's 'The Canterbury Tales' contains elements of much that was to follow – the drama, the novel, the short story, even today's television series. After all, they used much the same formula years later for the never-arriving 'Wagon Train'.

If Chaucer was alive today he'd be topping the ratings with a soap called 'Pilgrims' . . .

Chapter Two

WILLIAM SHAKESPEARE
1564–1616

All-Time Champ

Next comes our all-time superstar, the immortal Will Shakespeare. From sonnets to comedies to epic tragedies, nobody did it better – in fact, no one did it half as well. Probably the finest writer in the world . . .

The Kid from Stratford

Shakespeare was born in Stratford-upon-Avon, son of a local glovemaker. A bit of a tearaway as a lad, he once got nicked for poaching deer. He eventually married a local lady called Anne Hathaway.

'I wish you weren't so ambitious William and just stole apples like a normal little boy!'

Shakespeare Takes the Stage

Pretty soon Shakespeare left Stratford, and made his way to Elizabethan London, where the theatre was booming. After a brief career as a horse holder – a form of early parking attendant – he joined the Globe Theatre Players as an extra, and worked his way up to occasional small-part actor, then full-time poet and playwright.

After a long and successful career, he retired to his native Stratford, inherited his father's coat-of-arms, and ended his days as a real gentleman.

Pure Genius

Shakespeare wrote about thirty-seven plays, give or take the odd tragedy. You can spend a life-time studying Shakespeare – so here are some edited highlights.

The Play's the Thing

The plays can be divided into three main groups – history, tragedy and comedy. (Sometimes the groups overlap and you get a sort of tragi-comedy, as in 'The Winter's Tale'.)

There are the English history plays, dealing with the power struggles of the aristocracy, who used up any energy left after battling the French and other assorted Continentals in fighting each other.

The most famous propaganda job is 'Henry V':

'Once more unto the breach, dear friends, once more
Or close the wall up with our English dead.'

('Henry V' was famously filmed by Olivier – who's now been posthumously upstaged by Ken Branagh.)

This Scepter'd Isle

In 'Richard II' we get a riveting portrait of an evil, but not totally unlikeable, king, and an unforgettable speech in praise of England:

'This royal throne of Kings, this scepter'd isle
This earth of Majesty, this seat of Mars
This other Eden, demi-paradise
This fortress built by nature for herself
Against infection and the hand of war
This happy breed of men, this little world
This precious stone set in the silver sea . . .
This blessed plot, this earth, this realm
This England . . .'

(Something tells me our Will was no new European.)

No Place Like Rome

Then there are the great plays about Roman history. 'Julius Caesar':

'Beware the Ides of March!'

And 'Antony and Cleopatra', one of the world's great love stories:

*'Age cannot wither her nor custom stale
Her infinite variety.'*

Some Terrific Tragedies

There are the great tragedies. (Tragedy is often described as the story of some great man, brought low by a fatal flaw.)
'Romeo and Juliet' is the story of two
'star-crossed lovers' kept apart by their
feuding families:

*'But soft! what light through yonder window
breaks?
It is the east, and Juliet is the sun . . .'*

'King Lear' tells of an aging monarch who
divides his kingdom between two of his
daughters, Goneril and Regan – and
discovers too late that it is the neglected
Cordelia, who really loves him:

*'How sharper than a serpent's tooth it is
To have a thankless child!'*

'Othello' is the story of a man destroyed by
jealousy:

*'Oh beware my lord of jealousy
It is the green-eyed monster which doth mock
The meat it feeds on.'*

*'...Just rehearsing a bit of
Romeo and Juliet Miss!'*

The Scottish Play

'Macbeth' is a brave soldier ruined by a supernatural doom that plays on his ambition and that of his wife and leads him to murder the rightful king. Lady Macbeth, an early feminist, is quite willing to do the dirty deed herself when her husband hesitates:

'Infirm of purpose! Give me the daggers!'

7

Unhappy Hamlet

In the most tragic of all, 'Hamlet', the melancholy Danish prince is tipped off by his father's ghost that he's been murdered:

> *'Murder most foul, as in the best it is;*
> *But this most foul, strange and unnatural.'*

Hamlet takes the whole play to work himself up to avenging the murder, which was carried out by Hamlet's Uncle Claudius, who's since married his mother – Hamlet's mother, not Claudius's. To put it mildly:

> *'Something is rotten in the state of Denmark.'*

Needless to say, the lad comes up trumps in the end, and the play finishes with the stage positively littered with bodies.

Blood and Thunder

Shakespeare even descended to at least one splatter play. The heroine of 'Titus Andronicus' is raped and has her tongue and hands cut off. In revenge, her father serves the attackers' mother a pie made of her children's heads. To be fair, this is a very early work, written in collaboration – with Stephen King maybe? Scorned by critics, it was a smash-hit on stage at the time.

'Is there a Doctor in the house?'

Anything for a laugh

Then there are the comedies – 'Much Ado About Nothing', 'As You Like It', 'Twelfth Night', 'The Merchant of Venice' and 'A Midsummer Night's Dream'.

'There are fairies at Bottom's garden!'

It's interesting to note the way changing attitudes affect how we see the comedies today. The villain of 'The Merchant of Venice', the Jewish merchant Shylock, is now seen as one of Shakespeare's great tragic heroes.

'Hath not a Jew eyes? Hath not a Jew hands, organs, senses, dimensions, affections, passions? Fed with the same food, hurt with the same weapons, subject to the same diseases, healed by the same means, warmed and cooled by the same winter and summer as a Christian? If you prick us, do we not bleed? If you tickle us, do we not laugh? If you poison us, do we not die? And if you wrong us, shall we not revenge?'

No Way to Treat a Lady

Feminist critics turn mental somersaults trying to prove Shakespeare didn't really approve of events in 'The Taming of the Shrew'. Petruchio, the ultimate Male Chauvinist Pig, bullies and brainwashes the rebellious Kate into submission:

'She shall watch all night
And if she chance to nod, I'll rail and brawl
And with the clamour, keep her still awake
This is the way to kill a wife with kindness.'

At the end of the play the defeated Katherine grovels:

> '*Thy husband is thy lord, thy life, thy keeper,*
> *Thy head, thy sovereign, one that cares for thee . . .*'

(I don't think she means a word of it – and neither did Shakespeare!)

A Fine Romance

Finally come the three great Romances: 'Cymbeline', 'The Winter's Tale' and last of all 'The Tempest' in which the old magician, Prospero, lays down his magic staff for the last time – foreshadowing Shakespeare's approaching retirement:

> '*Our revels now are ended. These our actors*
> *As I foretold you were all spirits and are melted*
>   *into air, into thin air.*
> *And, like the baseless fabric of this vision,*
> *The cloud-capped towers, the gorgeous palaces*
> *The solemn temples, the great globe itself*
> *Yea, all which it inherit shall dissolve*
> *And, like this insubstantial pageant faded*
> *Leave not a rack behind. We are such stuff*
> *As dreams are made on, and our little life*
> *Is rounded with a sleep . . .*'

Ariel – nip down to McDonald's and get me a Big Mac!

Something for Everyone

Shakespeare provided his public with an amazingly varied diet. History, tragedy, comedy, plenty of blood and thunder, and always a good death-scene for the star.

What's more, his plays are director-proof. Set them in Victorian England, Mussolini's Italy, or an underwater tank with the actors in scuba-masks – and someone, usually Jonathan Miller, invariably does – the plays still work. The poetry, the imagery, the description of human emotion and character are all unrivalled.

An Occupation for Gentlemen

Interestingly enough, writing plays was considered rather low at the time – rather like writing for television today.

The proper occupation for a literary gent was poetry. The most fashionable sort was the sonnet, written to a strict fourteen-line form, ending in a rhyming couplet.

Shakespeare wrote 154 sonnets in all, and they express the whole range of human emotions.

You're the Greatest – and So Am I!

There's ecstatic young love:

'Shall I compare thee to a summer's day?
Thou art more lovely and more temperate
Rough winds do shake the darling buds of May . . .'

(Yes, that's where the title of H.E. Bates's book and the subsequent telly series comes from – people are always pinching Shakespeare's best lines.)

The sonnet ends with a breathtaking piece of poetic arrogance:

'So long as men can breath or eyes can see
So long lives this – and this gives life to thee.'

Love Hurts . . .

Other sonnets show savage disillusion:

'The expense of spirit in a waste of shame
Is lust in action, and till action, lust
Is perjured, murderous, bloody, full of blame
Savage, extreme, rude, cruel, not to trust . . .'

(Translation; love's a bitch when it goes wrong – and it always does!)

The Best in the Business

Shakespeare was the great popular entertainer of his time – of all time really. Just a working hack, you might say – and a towering genius as well.

Chapter Three

DANIEL DEFOE
1661–1731

The Merry Monarch

Daniel Defoe was born in 1661 – the year after the English finally got fed up with the Puritans and their republic and invited the exiled monarch Charles II, soon to be known as 'The Merry Monarch', back to the throne.

Dan Moves Up-Market

Son of a Stoke Newington butcher called George Foe, young Daniel stuck on the 'De' bit himself, reckoning it sounded more classy. An ambitious lad, Daniel started life as a merchant, trading near London's Royal Exchange. It was an exciting life. Once, on a business trip, he got captured by Algerian pirates. They soon let him go though, perhaps on payment of a ransom.

Dead Cats for Daniel

Soon after this, he turned his hand to writing. A satirical pamphlet about 'Dissenters' (as nonconformists were called then) landed him in the pillory. Undeterred by the dead cats and rotting cabbages flung at him – what's a bad review or two after all – Defoe went on to write over five hundred books, poems, pamphlets and tracts.

Although his poetry is largely forgotten today, he had a neat line in satirical verse:

'Wherever God erects a house of prayer
The Devil also builds a chapel there
And 'twill be found upon examination
The latter has the larger congregation.'

Dan the Spy

Writing didn't seem to be making him rich, and Defoe, a Thatcher-ite entrepreneur before his time, often tried to find an easier way to make a living.

He was a secret agent for a time, and even descended to writing political pamphlets for the Tory government.

Doing the Business

He also tried a number of business schemes including an early form of marine insurance, and had a fairly disastrous go at raising civet cats – cat-like African mammals from which is obtained (don't ask how) – a strong-smelling yellowish substance used in making perfume. Nothing seemed to work out. He went bankrupt several times and occasionally landed in jail.

'Change your perfume Charlotte
–you're attracting cats!'

Daniel Picks a Winner

Eventually Daniel decided to stick with literature – but he was nearly sixty before he discovered his winning formula. Some fifteen years before, a Scottish sailor called Alexander Selkirk had survived alone for five years on a desert island before eventually being rescued. Coming across Selkirk's rather boring account of his ordeal, Defoe hi-jacked the story – and turned it into 'Robinson Crusoe'.

A Stirring Tale

Having pinched the story, he improved it no end. Crusoe's shipwreck is brilliantly described:

'. . . a raging wave, mountain-like, came rowling astern of us. It took us with such a fury that it overset the boat at once, and separating us as well from the boat as from one another gave us not hardly time to say Oh God! for we were swallowed up in a moment.'

Struggling to Survive

Crusoe's desperate struggle to survive with the aid of stores rescued from the wreck is told in such convincing detail that we feel we are on the island with him. After years of solitude, Crusoe realises he is not alone:

Footprints and Friday

The famous footprint in the sand, the attacks by bloodthirsty cannibals, the rescue of Man Friday – all this is pure Defoe. The book is written in a racy straightforward style that seems strangely modern even today.

'It could be Sue Lawley from "Desert Island Discs"!'

Robinson II

'Robinson Crusoe' was a great success, and Defoe rushed out a quick sequel, 'The Further Adventures . . .' which was equally popular.

Defoe realised he was onto a good thing. But there just weren't enough interesting memoirs about. Then, in a blinding flash, he saw the answer. He could make up stories of his own – and tell them as if they were true!

Inventing the Novel

Without realising it, he'd virtually invented the novel! Defoe continued in the same documentary style with 'Memoirs of a Cavalier' and 'Captain Singleton', the story of a famous pirate. He told their stories as if they were true. At the time, most people believed they were.

Moll's Memorable Memoirs

Defoe's second most famous novel is 'Moll Flanders' – and his eager readers could see what they were getting right from the title page:

The FORTUNES and MISFORTUNES
of The Famous MOLL FLANDERS
Who was born in NEWGATE PRISON
and during a life of continu'd Variety for Threescore Years . . .
was Twelve Year a Whore, five times a Wife
(whereof once to her own brother) Twelve Year a Thief
Eight Year a Transported Felon in Virginia
at last grew Rich, liv'd Honest and died a Penitent,
Written from her own Memorandums

Selling Sex and Scandal

No cinema poster could promise more – and Defoe gives the reader full value. 'Moll Flanders' is the tear-jerking tale of a young girl condemned to hang for theft. Because she is pregnant, Moll's sentence is changed to transportation. After many harrowing adventures at sea, in America and back in England (including the disconcerting discovery that one of her many husbands is really her brother), Moll survives to enjoy a prosperous old age and reflect on her wicked life.

'Grow up Susan and read something really steamy!'

More Steamy Stories

'Moll Flanders' was followed by 'A Journal of the Plague Year', 'Captain Jack' and 'Roxana', the story of a high class courtesan. Tougher and less of a victim than Moll Flanders, the beautiful and ruthless Roxana abandons her spendthrift husband and becomes the mistress of a French prince, an English lord, and finally of the king.

'Are you reading steamy stories again Brenda — or have you left the kettle on?'

True Confessions

Like all Defoe's stories, 'Roxana' is written in a straightforward, racy 'true confessions' style.

Defoe's exciting and varied life, combined with wide reading and a colourful imagination, enabled him to fill his tales with exotic adventures set anywhere from Africa to Russia. His easy natural style, together with his love of romance and fascination with low-life adventure, makes him one of the first and most successful of Eng Lit's great popular entertainers. Robinson Crusoe, has achieved the same mythic status as Robin Hood, King Arthur and Sherlock Holmes – one of those characters everybody knows.

Chapter Four

ALEXANDER POPE
1688–1744

Alexander Pope was born in the year King James II lost his throne. James had turned out to be too Catholic for his Protestant-minded subjects. In 1688 they chucked him out, replacing him with his nephew, an impeccably Protestant Dutchman called William of Orange.

Out of Town

This wasn't entirely good news for young Alexander Pope, who was born into a Catholic family. According to some daft new regulation, Catholics had to live over ten miles from London. Pope's father, a prosperous linen draper, bought a house in Windsor Forest. When Alexander grew up he was barred, as a Catholic, from going to University.

A Bad Beginning

Life dealt young Alexander a pretty bad hand from the beginning. He caught tuberculosis as a child. It affected his spine and stunted his growth. He didn't grow over four-foot six, and he was weak and spindly with a hunched back. His health was never very good, and he suffered from pain and headaches all his life. He once referred to: 'This long disease, my life . . .'

Alexander the Bright

A child-prodigy, young Alexander read widely in several languages,

17

teaching himself as he went along. His career as a satirist got off to an early start – he was expelled from school for writing a rude poem about the Headmaster. (The poem doesn't seem to have survived, which may be just as well!)

Pope Goes to Town

At fifteen he was sent off to London to add French and Italian to his Latin and Greek. There he hung out in London's famous Coffee Houses, haunts of the fashionable literary set.

'I think I better bring you decaffeinated Master Alexander!'

All this time chatting over the cappuccino wasn't wasted though. In 1707, with Pope still (just) a teenager, Jacob Tonson, a famous literary figure of the day, offered to publish some of his poetry. The lad was on his way.

Playing It Cool

The fashionable writers of the day were the 'Augustans', named after the so-called 'golden age' of the Roman Emperor Augustus. They were a gentlemanly lot, very keen on 'correctness', reason, balance, and keeping up the classical tradition. Nothing too wild or fancy, nothing over the top.

For the Augustans there was only one way to write verse – the 'heroic couplet', two rhyming lines of ten syllables each. Alexander Pope is the form's undisputed master, turning its limitations into strengths.

Living by the Rules

Pope's first major work, his 'Essay on Criticism' is Augustan to the core. It's a set of rules for writing and for art, all according to the very best Augustan standards.

'First follow Nature and your judgement frame,
By her just standard, which is still the same.'

The poem is full of still quoted or mis-quoted, lines.

'A little learning is a dangerous thing'
'To err is human, to forgive, divine'.

'For fools rush in, where angels fear to tread'.

So, too, is his later 'Essay on Man':

'Hope springs eternal in the human breast
Man never is, but always to be blessed'.

And:

'Know then thyself, presume not God to scan
The proper study of Mankind is Man'.

Everything for the Best

'Essay on Criticism' expresses a typically Augustan attitude to life:

'All nature is but art, unknown to thee;
All chance, direction which thou canst not see;
All discord, harmony not understood;
And partial evil, universal good;
And, spite of pride, in erring reason's spite,
One truth is clear, whatever is, is right.'

19

A Hairy Problem

Another famous poem, 'The Rape of the Lock' describes the endless carryings-on in society and even amongst the gods in the heavens when an impetuous lover dares to snip off a lock of the beautiful Belinda's hair:

> 'What dire offence from
>   am'rous causes springs,
> What mighty contests
>   rise from trivial things.'

Pope at the Top

By the time Pope was twenty-five, he was a leading figure in London's literary world. His success was sealed by his massive and masterly translation of 'The Iliad' and 'The Odyssey', the great works of the Greek poet Homer.

Handicapped by poor health, Pope led a restricted life. Despite a life-long attachment to a lady called Martha Blount, he never married. He never travelled abroad, and spent all his life in literary circles in and around London. This wasn't always as peaceful as it sounds.

Very Satirical

Pope wasn't just a calm and gracious Augustan poet. He was a satirist too, in the savage tradition that still continues in *Private Eye*. The 'Epistle to Arbuthnot' is full of vicious sideswipes at his enemies.

'Stop wishing you were down there Alexander. "Private Eye" manages very well without you!'

Poetry With a Punch

Addison, rival poet and essayist, is someone always ready to:

'Damn with faint praise, assent with civil leer,
And, without sneering, teach the rest to sneer.'

A nobleman called Lord Hervey was clobbered as well:

'Yet let me flap this bug with gilded wings
This painted child of dirt, that stinks and stings.'

Damning the Dunces

In another mock-epic poem, 'The Dunciad', Pope savaged poets, critics, and anyone else who'd offended him – and it was a pretty long list. But 'The Dunciad' is more than just an attack on Pope's now-forgotten enemies. Pope was attacking not only dunces but dullness. He saw stupidity itself as the real enemy. In the poem's magnificent conclusion sheer chaos overwhelms everything:

'Lo! thy dread Empire, CHAOS is restor'd
Light dies before thy uncreating word
Thy hand, great Anarch, lets the curtain fall
And Universal Darkness covers all.'

A Poet to Admire

Like other Augustans, Pope could sometimes sound pompous and complacent. When he was angry, he wrote with a pen dipped in acid. But he was a dedicated craftsman, perhaps the most truly classical of English poets. He wasn't always all that lovable – but then, look what he had to put up with. Trapped in a feeble, twisted, pain-racked body, he fought his way to literary greatness by sheer will-power. It's difficult not to admire him.

Chapter Five

ROBERT BURNS
1759–1796

'Scots wha ha'e' – and all that!

You couldn't ask for a bigger contrast than that between the prim and proper Pope and the roaring and rambunctious Robert Burns. Or, as the Scots pronounce it, Rrrrabbie Burrrrrns – with an unlimited number of rolling 'r's.

Burns was born in Alloway, Ayrshire, the son of a poor farmer. Sent to school at six, he was later taught at home by a travelling teacher, hired by a group of local families. Then, as now, the Scots were very keen on education.

Down on the Farm

Rabbie was the eldest son, and at fifteen he was working on the farm. He kept up his reading, and started to write poems himself. In between the poetry and the muckspreading he managed to find time for those activities popular with so many later writers – wine, women and song.

'Oh Rabbie – I love the way you roll your 'R's!'

From Lecherous Layabout to Promising Poet

Ten years later his father died and Robert and his brother rented a farm at nearby Mossgiel. By the time a couple of years had gone by, Rabbie was in deep trouble. Not only was the farm going down the drain, but he'd got not one, but two of the local maidens in the family way. Their fathers were after his blood and Rabbie seriously considered emigrating . . .

'Rabbie's particularly good at "couplets"!'

Luckily his poetry was getting a bit of a reputation by now and he managed to raise enough money to publish a volume of poems. The book, 'Poems, Chiefly in the Scottish Dialect', was a huge success and it saved Burns's bacon.

The Poet of the Plough

Burns became celebrated as 'the poet of the plough'. He was invited everywhere and became a huge success in fashionable Edinburgh society. In those days a successful poet had something of the status of today's pop stars. All this party-going didn't do much for his work. Most of his best poems were written in his farming days – before he became famous.

Rabbie Goes Home

Eventually Rabbie went home and did the decent thing by at least one of the maidens, a girl called Jean Armour. (By now she'd borne him not one but two sets of twins.) To help out, his posh Edinburgh friends wangled him a job as a customs inspector in Dumfries. In the years that followed he wrote little original poetry. However, he edited and partly wrote two song collections. 'A Select Collection of Original Scottish Airs' was followed by 'The Scots Musical Museum'. He also wrote the famous 'Tam o' Shanter', his own version of a famous traditional ghost story.

Scotland Forever

In 1796 he died of rheumatic fever – though for all true Scotsmen, Rabbie Burns will never die. Every year, all over Scotland, there are celebrations on his birthday. Never was a poet better remembered by his adoring countrymen.

In a way all this adulation has done Rabbie's reputation more harm than good. All the fuss and feasting, all the Burns Night Suppers with the pipers marching the haggis in, can make him seem part of the Scottish Tourist industry. (Though come to think of it, he did write a poem to the haggis.)

> *'Great Chieftain o' the puddin' race . . .'*

In fact Burns is a very fine poet with a considerable range of subjects and styles.

'I thought Rod Stewart was our oldest pop star!'

Ode to a Mouse

'To a Mouse – On Turning Her Up In Her Nest With the Plough' starts off in the broadest of Scots:

> *'Wee, sleekit, cowrin', tim'rous beastie,*
> *O, what a panic's in thy breastie!*
> *Thou needna start awa' sae hasty,*
> *Wi bick'ring brattle!* ('Bick'ring brattle' means 'hasty scamper'.)

The second verse is in formal poetic language:

> *'I'm truly sorry man's dominion*
> *Has broken Nature's social union*
> *And justifies that ill opinion*
> *Which mak's thee startle . . .'*

Of Mice and Morals

Burns makes us feel his sympathy for the poor mouse, left to face the cold winter without food and shelter. Then in some of his most

'By the way dear, are we up to date with the house insurance?'

famous lines he draws the moral. Men, just as much as mice, can fall victim to unexpected disaster:

'The best-laid schemes o' mice and men
Gang aft a-gley,
And lea'e us nought but grief and pain
For promised joy.'

Holy Willie

In 'Holy Willie's Prayer' he draws a brilliant portrait of a smugly religious hypocrite. 'Holy Willie' is convinced that he is saved while everyone else is damned. But he does have lapses:

'Oh Lord, yestreen, Thou kens, wi' Meg —
Thy pardon I sincerely beg . . .
An' I'll ne'er lift a lawless leg
Again upon her.'

(Is this the first legover in Eng Lit?)

'Is that by the same author as Wicked Willie?'

Songs of Love

And there are beautifully simple songs and poems about love:

'O my luve is like a red, red rose,
That's newly sprung in June.
O my luve is like the melodie
That's sweetly play'd in tune.'

The Immortal Rabbie

Burns is one of the few writers from genuinely humble beginnings to achieve lasting fame. He may have been over-fond of the drink and the ladies, and too easily led astray by the temptations of fame.

But for all that, he was warm-hearted and generous, an enemy of hypocrisy and a life-long champion of the delights of everyday life and the rights of ordinary people.

A man ahead of his time, he believed that it wasn't who you were but what you were that mattered.

'The rank is but the guinea's stamp
The man's the gowd for a' that
For a' that' and a' that
A man's a man for a' that!'

Chapter Six

WILLIAM WORDSWORTH
1770–1850

William Wordsworth, leader of that poetic Wild Bunch, the Romantic Poets, was born in Cumberland, third in a family of five. His dad was a lawyer, the legal agent of one of the local noblemen. William's mother died when he was eight, his father when he was thirteen. The kids were farmed out to various uncles, and William was separated from Dorothy, his favourite sister.

He was sent away to grammar school in Hawkshead, in the Lake District, lodging with a local family. The lonely lad spent a lot of time wandering around the wild and beautiful countryside, and developed a mystic love – and fear – of nature that was to influence him all his life.

A Fright in the Night

In his long, autobiographical poem 'The Prelude', Wordsworth tells how one night he was rowing a boat across a lake towards a craggy ridge. Suddenly:

'. . . *a huge peak, black and huge,*
As if with voluntary power instinct
Upreared its head.'

Terrified the boy rows away but:

'. . . *growing still in stature the grim shape*
Towered up between me and the stars, and still,
For so it seemed, with purpose of its own
And measured motion like a living thing
Strode after me.'

Not everyone gets chased by a mountain!

27

Wandering Willie

In 1787 William went to St John's College, Cambridge. He was a keen but erratic student, reading widely, usually books not on the course. He took a not very distinguished degree in 1791, visited London and Wales and then went off to France.

Up the Rebels!

All this was in the early days of the French Revolution, and young William, like other romantic young men of the time, saw the revolution as the beginning of a new age of freedom and justice. In a later poem he wrote:

'Bliss was it that dawn to be alive
But to be young was very heaven!'

(As long as you weren't a young aristo, headed for the chop!)

William in Love

During his time in France, William fell madly in love with a young lady called Annette Vallon, daughter of a surgeon in Blois. Soon it wasn't just William's revolutionary zeal that was swelling – Annette was enlarging as well.

'Dear Dorothy, Vivre La France and Liberty – especially with Annette!'

Parted by Fate

William was all set to marry Annette and join the revolutionaries in Paris. Not surprisingly his guardian uncles back home didn't approve of his plans. They refused to send any more money and William had to come home – leaving Annette behind. Just a few days later, their daughter Caroline was born. Soon England and France were at war, and any hope of rejoining Annette was gone.

William's Career

The next few years were unsettled and unhappy ones for young William. He was writing poetry by now and in 1793 he published 'Descriptive Sketches' an account of his Continental walking tour and another poem called 'An Evening Walk'.

A young friend died, leaving him a small legacy, and he was offered a rent-free cottage in Dorset. Setting up house with his beloved sister Dorothy, Wordsworth started life as a full-time poet. Later they moved to Alfoxden in Somerset, largely so Wordsworth could be nearer his new friend and collaborator, a colourful character called Coleridge. In 1798 the two poets produced 'Lyrical Ballads', an anonymous collaboration.

The Lake Poets

After a trip to Germany with Coleridge, William and Dorothy came home and settled down. This time they moved to Dove Cottage in Grasmere in the Lake District. (This is why Wordsworth, Coleridge, and their friend Southey are often called the Lake Poets – not, as some of their critics say, because they were all wet.)

THE LAKE POETS

Reunion with Annette

During a short truce in the unending war with France, William and Dorothy popped across the Channel to France to visit Annette Vallon and to see their daughter Caroline for the first time. The romance was obviously over. Soon after his return home, Wordsworth married Mary Hutchinson, a childhood friend. In time they were to have five children. (Not even marriage was allowed to part Wordsworth from his beloved sister, Dorothy. Even after he and Mary were married, Dorothy still lived with them – a sort of built-in Universal Aunt.) Over the years, Wordsworth's reputation grew steadily, even though his poetic powers declined.

Joining the Establishment

His revolutionary zeal gradually faded. Politically, like many another writer, he drifted slowly from Left to Right.

In 1813 Wordsworth was given the job of Distributor of Stamps for Westmorland with a salary of £400 a year – good money in those days. In 1842 he was given a Civil List pension of £300 a year. In 1843 he followed his friend Southey as Poet Laureate.

The Grand Old Man

By the end of his life, Wordsworth was the undisputed Grand Old Man of English Poetry. He died in 1850 when he was eighty – a good old age today, and an incredible one then. (For writers, particularly poets, the next best thing to dying romantically young is to live to be very, very old . . .)

A Poet's Philosophy

The basis of Wordsworth's poetic philosophy is spelt out, perhaps a bit pompously, in the Preface to 'Lyrical Ballads'.

> *'The principal object . . . was to choose incidents and situations from common life and to relate or describe them in a selection of language really used by men.'*

Here too, Wordsworth gives his famous definition of poetry:

> *'Poetry is the spontaneous overflow of powerful feelings: it takes its origin from emotion recollected in tranquillity.'*

Keeping it Simple

Wordsworth's use of simple themes and simple words can be magical:

> *'I wandered lonely as a cloud*
> *That floats on high o'er vales and hills*
> *When all at once I saw a crowd,*
> *A host, of golden daffodils.'*

There's the famous sonnet, 'Composed upon Westminster Bridge':

> *'Earth has not anything to show more fair*
> *Dull would he be of soul who could pass by*
> *A sight so touching in its majesty . . .'*

Simply Silly

Sometimes Wordsworth could drop with a thump into the ridiculous – as in some unfortunate lines about a puddle:

> *'I've measured it from side to side*
> *'Tis three feet long and two feet wide.'*

Or in that unlikely ode, 'To the Spade of a Friend' which begins:

> *'Spade! with which Wilkinson hath*
> *tilled his lands.'*

The Power and the Pathos

But there is no denying the power and the pathos of the lines in 'Intimations of Immortality' in which the poet laments the fading of his youthful poetic vision:

> *'There was a time when meadow, grove and stream*
> *The earth, and every common sight*
> *To me did seem*
> *Apparelled in celestial light*
> *The glory and the freshness of a dream.*
> *It is not now as it hath been of yore;–'*

William's Masterpiece

This theme recurs in Wordsworth's greatest and longest poem, 'The Prelude'. It was published soon after his death and is undoubtedly his masterpiece. (So it should be – he was working on it for forty years!)

'The Prelude' is a sort of spiritual autobiography, something previously quite unknown in literature. In it Wordsworth shows 'the growth of a poet's mind'. He tries to recapture and define his mystic, youthful vision of the natural world – a vision already beginning to fade:

> *'The days gone by*
> *Come back upon me from the dawn almost*
> *Of life: the hiding places of my power*
> *Seem open: I approach, and then they close*
> *I see by glimpses now: when age comes on*
> *May scarcely see at all . . .'*

Poet and Preacher

At his worst, William Wordsworth can be boring, preachy, and unbearably long-winded. At his best, his poetry is wonderfully simple – and simply wonderful.

Like one of the massive brooding crags of his beloved Lake District, Wordsworth is a towering landmark in English poetry.

Chapter Seven

SAMUEL TAYLOR COLERIDGE
1772–1834

Samuel Taylor Coleridge was born in Ottery St Mary in Devon, youngest of a family of ten. His father John Coleridge was the vicar – and the local schoolmaster as well.

Sam was an infant prodigy from the cradle, a great reader, and a brilliant talker, soaking up Greek and Latin like a sponge.

Sam Goes To College

At nineteen, Coleridge entered Jesus College, Cambridge. For the first two years everything went well. Sam worked hard, and won a prize for poetic composition. He also became interested in politics – like many students he was a keen revolutionary. In his third year, however, he went right off the rails.

Sam Goes Wild

The trouble started when he fell madly in love with a young lady called Mary Evans. Unfortunately, she didn't feel anything like the same enthusiasm for him. Sam started whooping it up and drowning his sorrows. Soon he was badly in debt as well. He began to take laudanum – liquid opium – mixed with brandy, to help with his rheumatism.

'I've dishcovered a cure for rheumatishm!'

Soldier Sam

On a sudden mad impulse, Sam ran away from college and joined the army. He enlisted in a cavalry regiment, the Fifteenth Light Dragoons, under the unlikely name of Silas Tomkin Comberbach. Clumsy and scruffy at the same time, Sam was far from a born soldier – and the Dragoons didn't have much use for a trooper who could spout Latin and Greek but kept falling off his horse.

It was a relief for everyone concerned when Sam's family tracked him down and got him out – under a sort of insanity clause. His college forgave him but Sam couldn't settle down again. In 1794 he left without taking a degree, and lived in Bristol. He met Robert Southey (later to become Poet Laureate) and in 1795 married Sara Fricker, a friend of Southey's. He also met Wordsworth, beginning the great friendship of his life. A friend of Coleridge's found him a cottage at Nether Stowey in the Quantock Hills. The Wordsworths moved to nearby Alfoxden, and the two poets began their collaboration on 'Lyrical Ballads'.

Wedgwood to the Rescue

Then, as now, there wasn't much money in poetry and Coleridge kept going by writing articles for the 'Morning Post'.

'The Church appeals to me – nice uniform and no need to ride horses!'

He was seriously thinking about joining the Church – he'd have been a bigger disaster as a vicar than as a soldier – when he had a sudden stroke of luck. The wealthy Wedgwood brothers, makers of the famous pottery, offered him an annuity of a hundred and fifty pounds a year for life, so he could devote himself to being a full-time poet.

34

Sam's Poetic Hat-Trick

It was money well spent. Coleridge wrote some of his best work at this time – including the three great poems for which he is best remembered. Perhaps the most famous of the three is that amazing ballad 'The Ancient Mariner'.

Written in a deliberately old-fashioned style it tells of a poor soul who gets nabbed on his way to a wedding by the old salt of the title.

'By thy long grey beard and glittering eye
Now wherefore stopps't thou me?'

He soon finds out.

'He holds him with his skinny hand
"There was a ship" quoth he.'

Rather unkindly the Wedding Guest replies:

'Hold off! Unhand me, grey-beard loon!'

The old sailor lets go, but:

'He holds him with his glittering eye
He cannot choose but hear.'

All at Sea

The whiskery old codger spins him an amazing yarn about a doomed voyage on a cursed ship. The trouble comes when an albatross starts following the ship.

'"God save thee, Ancient Mariner,
From the fiends that plague thee thus!–
Why look'st thou so?" – "With my crossbow
I shot the Albatross."'

The Endangered Albatross

After this attack on an endangered species nothing goes right! The ship is becalmed:

'As idle as a painted ship
Upon a painted ocean.'

They run out of water:

'Water, water, everywhere,
And all the boards did shrink;
Water, water, everywhere
Nor any drop to drink.'

The Mariner's Message

Everyone dies, except the Mariner himself. After many more amazing and supernatural adventures, including an encounter with a ghost-ship, he survives and is finally rescued.

But now for penance, he must roam the world, telling his story to those that need to hear his message:

'He prayeth well who loveth well,
Both bird and man and beast.'

'Now promise me you'll stay away from elderly sailors!'

After delivering possibly the first conservation commercial in English Literature, the Mariner disappears. The Wedding Guest staggers home stunned.

'A sadder and a wiser man
He rose the morrow morn.'

Creepy 'Christabel'

'Christabel' is another weird medieval-style ballad. It's midnight in a spooky old castle. The Baron's daughter, the beautiful young Christabel, has gone to the nearby wood to pray for her 'betrothed knight'. There she sees a mysterious figure in white. The lady, Geraldine, claims to have been kidnapped. Christabel takes her back to the castle and gives her shelter. As they undress for bed, Christabel sees something strange and horrible about Geraldine:

'Behold! her bosom and half her side –
A sight to dream of, not to tell.'

Exactly what Geraldine's problem is, we never quite learn. (Maybe her silicon implant's exploded!) But it's clear that there's something spooky about her, and that Christabel is in danger.

'O shield her! Shield sweet Christabel.'

Since the story is unfinished, we never do find out exactly what's going on.

The Immortal Dream

Probably the best-known of all Coleridge's works is the famous 'Kubla Khan'. The poem is an opium dream. Coleridge had taken a few drops of opium to 'ward off an attack of dysentery'. (If this unlikely tale is true 'Kubla Khan' is the only great poem in literature to owe its origin to an attack of the trots.)

The unfinished poem tells how:

KUBLA KHAN
(The original manuscript)

'In Xanadu did Kubla Khan
A stately pleasure-dome decree
Where Alph, the sacred river, ran
Through caverns measureless to man
Down to a sunless sea.'

(Alf always struck me as being a funny name for a river.)

Vividly the poem describes a splendid, savage landscape.

'But oh! that deep, romantic chasm which slanted
Down the green hill athwart a cedarn cover
A savage place! as holy and enchanted
As e'er beneath a waning moon was haunted
By woman wailing for her demon lover!'

Sam's New Romance

Sam was doing well with his poetry, but his personal life was a disaster. Although he was already married, he fell madly in love with Sara Hutchinson, sister of Wordsworth's fiancée, Mary. Soon Coleridge's marriage was definitely on the rocks. The damp climate of the lakes made Coleridge's rheumatism worse, and he turned more and more to his favourite opium and brandy cocktail for relief.

Sam Seeks the Sun

Leaving the damp and gloomy lakes – and his damp and gloomy wife – Coleridge went off to sunny Malta, where he worked for a while as the Governor's secretary. He came back to London, delivered a course of lectures on philosophy, and then returned to the Lake District. Increasingly unstable, he quarrelled with Wordsworth and went back to London. Coleridge led an increasingly rackety life after that. He still managed to write and lecture. But his behaviour was erratic, his health was terrible, and the brandy and opium addiction stronger than ever.

The Saving of Sam

By this time Coleridge definitely needed a doctor. Luckily, that's exactly what he got. An old friend, Dr James Gillman took him in. For the rest of his life Coleridge became a sort of resident patient, living with the Gillmans in Highgate. Dr Gillman got Coleridge's opium addiction under control, and gradually his health began to improve. He was able to get on with his philosophical and critical work, and wrote a number of books. In 1828 he made up with Wordsworth, and they even made a trip to the Rhine together.

Sam the Sage

In the years that followed Coleridge wrote several more important books of philosophy and criticism. Trendy young intellectuals from all over London flocked to the Gillmans' house to listen to the wise words of 'The Sage of Highgate'. Rather like his own 'Ancient Mariner', Coleridge held them spellbound with a stream of brilliant talk.

By the time he died in 1834, Coleridge was widely regarded as one of the great men of his time. Wordsworth said he was 'the most wonderful man I have ever known'.

Today Coleridge is best remembered for the three weird and compelling poems he wrote when he was young – 'The Ancient Mariner', 'Christabel' and 'Kubla Khan' – and the last two aren't even finished!

Chapter Eight

JANE AUSTEN
1775–1817

Plain Jane

No steamy revelations here – not a lot happened in Jane Austen's quiet, respectable life. She was born in a little village in Hampshire, fifth in a family of seven children. (Well, they had to make their own amusements in those days.) Her father was a clergyman, not rich but with wealthy relatives. Jane spent her time at home with her family, enjoying the simple pleasures of country life: walks, visits to and from neighbours, the odd dinner-party. The only real excitement was provided by occasional balls, private dances in the houses of the local gentry. (There's a story of an older lady who finds a group of young girls chattering excitedly. 'There you are, my dears,' she says. 'Talking balls as usual!')

'I bought him from a sailor who must have been keen on dancing!'

All Human Life

Over the years, Jane Austen was to write six novels. You might wonder what she found to write about. The answer, of course, was everyday life. Parents, family, friends, funny neighbours, local feuds. Above all, she wrote about romance.

'When you say you're marrying a good man do you mean good'n rich or good'n bed?'

In those days marriage was the *only* career for a woman. It was vital to catch a good husband. 'Good' meant of good family, well-born – and equally important, well-off. The tone is perfectly caught by the first sentence of 'Pride and Prejudice':

'It is a truth universally acknowledged, that a single man in possession of a good fortune must be in want of a wife.'

Love and Money

Love, marriage and money are central to all six of Jane Austen's novels. Under the keen eyes of family and friends her heroines flirt, form attachments, get engaged, and eventually get married. On the way, there are lovers' tiffs and occasional disasters. Rash engagements are made and later broken. Some girls fall for cads and bounders, and even elope with them! Everything ends happily in respectable marriage.

A Quiet Life

Jane Austen herself never married. She was never considered a beauty, and worse still, she was very intelligent. As Jane herself said: 'A woman, especially if she have the misfortune of knowing anything, should conceal it as best she can.' She did have her admirers. One proposed and Jane actually accepted – only to change her mind next day. She spent the rest of her life with her family. When her father retired, they moved for a while to Bath. Although Jane often used the fashionable town in her novels, she was never really happy there. When her father died, Jane's brother Edward offered her and her mother a cottage on his estate. Here Jane wrote her last three novels, and spent her days as a maiden aunt, much loved by her many nephews and nieces. She died, still in her early forties, of 'a wasting disease'.

Six Splendid Stories

Despite their conventional romantic plots, Jane Austen's six novels are still remembered and, more important, still read today. The main reason lies in the sheer elegance and precision of the language – Jane Austen was simply one of the best writers around. Reading her prose is like hearing a fine instrument, skilfully played by a master. Her characters are beautifully drawn, not only the heroines, but the minor figures as well. The novels provide a devastatingly accurate, bitingly satirical picture of one small section of English life.

Sense and Sensibility

This is the story of a hard-up widow, Mrs Dashwood, and her daughters, Elinor and Marianne. Elinor is quiet and sensible, Marianne high-flown and romantic. Both girls fall in love, both romances go wrong. Elinor behaves with quiet dignity, hiding her sorrow. Marianne does the full tragedy-queen:

'Misery such as mine has no pride. I care not who knows that I am wretched.'

It's easy to see who gets Jane's sympathy.

'The trouble with being lovers in a Jane Austen novel means we'll end up marrying somebody else!'

Pride and Prejudice

This has always been the most popular of Jane Austen's novels. High-born haughty hero looks down on the heroine at first, and then, humbled, comes to love her:

'In vain have I struggled. It will not do. My feelings will not be repressed. You must allow me to tell you how ardently I admire and love you.'

Turned off by his unfeeling arrogance, our heroine turns him down. Nevertheless, the charming and high-spirited Elizabeth Bennet and the proud and haughty Fitzwilliam Darcy – there's a name for a romantic hero – eventually find happiness together.

Mansfield Park

This is a family saga in which the children of the Bertram family, and idealistic Fanny Price, the little girl they have taken in, grow up and face the problems of life.

Emma

Of 'Emma' Jane Austen said: 'I am going to take a heroine whom no-one but myself will much like.'

Emma Woodhouse is certainly snobbish, conceited and self-centred. She tries to run, and nearly ruins, her humble friend Harriet's life. But Emma's heart is in the right place. By the end of the novel she learns her lesson, and marries the eminently-sensible Mr Knightley.

Northanger Abbey

Northanger Abbey contains rather more action than the other novels – though much of it takes place inside the dizzy young heroine's head. It's a send-up of the Gothic horror novels with which young Catherine Morland frightens herself into fits. When she visits the sinister family seat of her new friend Eleanor Tilney, she imagines all kinds of ghastly secrets. But much to her disappointment, she finally realises that General Tilney, Eleanor's widowed father, *hasn't* murdered his late wife. He isn't even keeping her locked in the attic, secretly still alive . . .

Persuasion

The last, and perhaps the most touching of all Jane Austen's stories. Some time before it begins, Anne Elliot has been 'persuaded' to break off her engagement to Frederick Wentworth, a young naval officer.

Years later, he re-appears in her life, a prosperous and successful Captain. Anne still loves him.

'All the privilege I claim for my own sex is that of loving longest, when existence or when hope is gone.'

The tone of 'Persuasion' is less satirical and more tender than

Jane's other novels. Even though her own romance didn't work out, she could still give Anne's a happy ending . . .

Two Inches of Ivory

Jane Austen herself said that: 'Three or four families in a country village is the very thing to work on.'

She compared her work to: 'The little bit "two inches wide" of ivory on which I work with so fine a brush.'

Her range of personal experience was strictly limited – but no-one could have made better use of it. In her own way, this quiet and modest maiden lady is one of the giants of English Literature.

'I hate Jane Austen
– she supported the Ivory Trade!'

Chapter Nine

GEORGE GORDON, LORD BYRON
1788–1824

Our next poet, although still a Romantic – boy, was he Romantic – is a very different type from Wordsworth, Coleridge and the rest of the nature boys. Born to an aristocratic family, he was the son of a penniless younger son, who'd fled abroad to escape his creditors and died in disgrace. Left penniless, Byron's mother brought him home to Aberdeen, where they lived as despised poor relations on the fringes of their noble and wealthy family.

Byron's Lucky Break

Suddenly everything changed. The heir to the title was killed in action, the current title-holder popped off as well. At ten years old, George was the Sixth Lord Byron, the head of the family. All he inherited, besides the title, was the family seat, Newstead Abbey, which was in ruins, and the family estate, loaded with debts.

Education of a Poet

Toughened by his early hardships, young George grew up a lively high-spirited lad with a keen interest in the opposite sex. (He's said to have made an early start with his nursemaid.) In 1801 he went off

'Hop into bed Nanny, it's time I took a keen interest in the opposite sex!'

to Harrow which was a tough place in those days. Byron survived pretty well. Despite his disability – he'd been born with a club-foot – he was a keen athlete and a good boxer. At seventeen he went on to Cambridge, more interested in writing poetry and having a good time than in study – in any case, his noble rank entitled him to 'a degree without examination.'

Weight-watcher Byron

His other main worry was his weight. He was good-looking, but he did have a tendency to put it on a bit. A tubby romantic hero is out of the question. Byron fought the battle of the bulge with diet and exercise all his life.

'Run faster – I need the exercise!'

Early Works

His first volume of poetry, 'Fugitive Pieces', caused a scandal, since it included some satirical and some erotic poems. Byron replaced it with 'Hours of Idleness', a cleaned-up version with the naughty poems replaced by soppy ones. It didn't do him much good. The volume was carved up by the 'Edinburgh Review'. Byron fought back with another poem, 'English Bards and Scotch Reviewers.'

'I'll publish, right or wrong:
Fools are my theme, let satire be my song.'

Score, one-all.

Home and Away

Leaving university, Byron went off on the standard Grand Tour, visiting Spain, Portugal and Greece, which was still under Turkish

'Lock up your daughters – Byron's coming – pass it on!'

rule. On his return to England, he took his seat in the House of Lords, kicking-off with a stunning speech in support of the Nottingham textile workers. The poor in England, he said, were worse off than those abroad. The speech made him well-known in fashionable society.

Then he published 'Childe Harold' the long narrative poem he'd written on his travels, and, as he said himself, 'awoke one morning and found myself famous.'

Byron the Superstar

'Childe' is an old-fashioned word for a young nobleman, and 'Childe Harold' is the story of a young man's travels in search of adventure. It was dramatic:

> *'War, war, is still the cry, – "War, even to the knife!"'*

and nostalgic about the lost glory of Greece:

> *'Fair Greece! sad relic of departed worth!*
> *Immortal though no more: though fallen, great!'*

The poem was an instant success – and there was almost as much interest in the aristocratic young poet as in the poetry.

Rich and Famous

Byron's poetry didn't just make him famous, it made him rich. 'Childe Harold' was a best seller, and when his publisher offered one thousand five hundred pounds for another 'canto' as the instalments were called, Byron coolly insisted on two thousand five hundred – an incredible sum in those days. For the next few years he led the life of a poetic pop star. Fashionable hostesses were delighted to have him – and not just for dinner. More chased than chasing, he had numerous love-affairs, including a very public fling with the notorious Lady Caroline Lamb. (Less public at first, but ultimately far more damaging, was his rumoured affair with a married lady called Augusta Leigh – who just happened to be his half-sister.)

'I had Byron for dinner.'

'I had Byron for breakfast!'

The One Year Marriage

Despite his high earnings, Byron's debts were growing even higher. His friends urged him to nab a wealthy heiress, and in 1815 he married Annabella Milbanke. She wasn't just rich she was well educated and high-principled as well, and she tried to reform him.

She didn't have much luck. Byron refused to give up drink and low company – and he refused to stop seeing Augusta. A year later Annabella took their new-born baby daughter back home to mum.

Out of Favour

Public sympathy sided with Annabella. There were rumours that Byron was actually insane, and the shocking story of his affair with Augusta was leaking out. Suddenly Byron was an outcast from society. Defiantly he went off on his travels – and started writing another canto of 'Childe Harold.' He really was a romantic exile now.

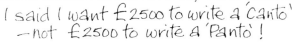

I said I want £2500 to write a 'Canto' – not £2500 to write a 'Panto' !

Byron in Exile

He rented a villa by Lake Geneva, and struck up a friendship with Shelley, another exiled poet. He had an affair with Shelley's wife's half-sister, Claire Clairmont, who bore him a daughter, Allegra.

Eventually Claire went back to England with the Shelleys. Byron moved on to Italy. Selling Newstead Abbey to clear his debts, he ended up in Venice where he began his greatest work, 'Don Juan' and his 'last attachment' – an affair with a young Italian noble-woman, Teresa Guiccioli, the wife of an elderly Count.

Greek Freedom Again

By 1822 they were living together in Genoa. Byron was approached by the London Greek Committee, and he agreed to help in the struggle for Greek freedom. Leaving Teresa, he sailed for Greece, eventually ending up in a small fishing-port called Missolonghi.

A Heroic Failure

As usual the Greeks were squabbling amongst themselves and arguing with their European advisers. Byron tried to pull things together, but before anything practical could be achieved, he caught a fever and died. His death did much to rally European opinion to the Greek cause. Eventually the Greeks regained their freedom – and Byron is still a hero in Greece today.

Songs of Love

Byron's colourful life tends to overshadow his work. He wrote some wonderful poetry – not so much the early romantic tosh that made his name but the simpler love lyrics:

'She walks in beauty like the night
Of cloudless climes and starry skies;
And all that's best of dark and bright
Meet in her aspect and her eyes.'

There's Byron's touching farewell to romantic adventure:

'So we'll go no more a-roving
So late into the night,
Though the heart be still as loving
And the moon be still as bright.
For the sword outwears its sheath,
And the soul wears out the breast,
And the heart must pause to breathe,
And love itself have rest.'

Above all there's his final master-work, 'Don Juan', a rambling witty narrative poem, full of outrageous rhymes:

'But – Oh! ye lords of ladies intellectual
Inform us truly, have they not hen-pecked you all?'

And outrageous sentiments:

'What men call gallantry and gods adultery
Is much more common where the climate's sultry.'
'Pleasure's a sin – and sometimes sin's a pleasure.'

Most significant of all, in view of Byron's eventual fate:

'The mountains look on Marathon –
And Marathon looks on the sea;
And musing there an hour alone,
I dreamed that Greece might still be free.'

It's somehow typical of Byron that after an existence devoted to selfish, sensual pleasure, he died alone in a distant land, sacrificing his life for a cause that was not his own.

Chapter Ten

PERCY BYSSHE SHELLEY
1792–1822

Romantic Revolutionary

Percy Bysshe Shelley was the son of a Member of Parliament, and the grandson of a baronet. He was sent to Eton – which is where all the trouble started. Public schools were tough in those days. (When the Duke of Wellington said, 'Waterloo was won on the playing fields of Eton' he meant that if you were tough enough to survive Eton, fighting in a major battle was a piece of cake.)

'I'm glad I never went to school at Eton mate!'

Shelly's Schooldays

Poor Shelley didn't stand a chance. He was intellectual, poetic and sensitive, he hated games, he had long golden curls and his first name was Percy. Nicknamed 'Mad Shelley', he was constantly bullied. His school-fellows were fond of 'Shelley-hunting' – a wild chase with Shelley as the fox. Not surprisingly, Shelley became a rebel. He had already started his career as a poet, publishing 'Zastrozzi: A Romance' while still at school.

'Go and find your own fox hole!'

Shelley's Rebellion

At Oxford Shelley played the role of poetic rebel, dressing and behaving in a deliberately offensive way. But he went too far when he co-wrote an anti-religious pamphlet, 'The Necessity of Atheism'. They took religion seriously in those days. Shelley was promptly expelled.

Back home he lost no time in getting into more trouble. Harriet Westbrook, a sixteen-year-old friend of his sister's was unhappy with her family. Shelley decided to 'rescue' her, and they eloped to Edinburgh.

A Wandering Poet

Shelley led a wandering life for the next few years, dodging creditors, quarrelling with Harriet, who bore him two children, and writing 'Queen Mab', a revolutionary philosophical poem. By now Shelley had found a fellow spirit in the Radical philosopher (and apostle of free love) William Godwin. He soon put theory into practice by running off with Godwin's sixteen-year-old daughter Mary.

Shelley Abroad

They travelled in Europe for some time, then returned to England when Shelley's grandfather died, leaving him £1000 a year. They lived in Windsor for a while, returning to Lake Geneva in the summer of 1816. Shelley became friends with the exiled Byron, and Mary wrote her still-remembered Gothic romance, 'Frankenstein', which later inspired countless horror movies.

'This gentleman wants a word with you about your new book Mary!'

That same summer poor Harriet drowned herself in the Serpentine, and Shelley and Mary were married.

Home and Away

They returned to England again, but things didn't work out. Despite his inheritance, Shelley was still in debt. In 1818 Shelley and his second family – there were two more kids by now – made off to Italy. Behind him, Shelley left a pile of unpaid bills and his most famous sonnet, 'Ozymandias' – which probably wasn't much consolation to his creditors.

The Shelleys wandered restlessly round Italy. By now the marriage was showing signs of strain. Tragically, their daughter, Clara, died in Venice, and soon afterwards their son died in Rome. Mary had a nervous breakdown. She recovered and gave birth to another son, and the Shelleys finally settled down close to Pisa.

'Life hasn't exactly been on the level for us, has it Mary?'

The Poet at Work

Through all these troubled times, Shelley was hard at work, producing an amazing variety of poetry. He wrote two long poetic dramas, 'Prometheus Unbound' and 'The Cenci', the famous 'Ode to the West Wind', numerous other odes on political themes, and many outstanding lyric poems. But he found it hard to get his poems published in England, where he was still seen as an immoral revolutionary atheist and general bad lot.

Love and Sailing

Shelley's love life was as complicated as ever. He fell in love with a beautiful Italian girl, Emilia, and with Jane, the wife of his friend Edward Williams, writing passionate poems to them both. During his time in Italy, Shelley had developed a passion for sailing, even though he'd never learned to swim. He'd just bought his own boat, a little schooner called 'Ariel'.

The Final Drama

In August 1822, Shelley, Williams and a boat-boy, sailed along the coast to nearby Livorno, to visit Byron. On the way back, the little schooner was caught in a summer storm, and sank with all hands. The bodies were washed up later. Because of the local quarantine laws they were burned on the beach. In a scene as dramatic as any in Shelley's poetic dramas, Byron stood watching by the blazing funeral-pyre of his drowned friend.

Poetry of Many Kinds

Shelley's poetry is amazingly varied. There are long, eloquent passages filled with poetic images:

'O wild West Wind, thou breath of Autumn's being
Thou from whose unseen presence the leaves dead
Are driven like ghosts from an enchanter fleeing.'

There's the famous 'To a Skylark':

'Hail to thee, blithe spirit!
Bird thou never wert,
That from heaven or near it
Pourest thy full heart . . .'

There are simpler lyrics:

To a Skylark

'Music, when soft verses die,
Vibrates in the memory.'

and:

'When the lamp is shattered
The light in the dust lies dead.'

There is savage political satire, like the verses attacking the reactionary politician Lord Castlereagh.

'I met Murder in the way
He had a mask, like Castlereagh.'

Best remembered of all Shelly's poems is the sonnet 'Ozymandias'. In one devastatingly simple image, Shelley shows the downfall of the tyranny he hated and fought all his life.

'*I met a traveller from an antique land*
Who said: "Two vast and trunkless legs of stone
Stand in the desert. Near them, on the sand,
Half sunk, a shattered visage lies . . .
And on the pedestal these words appear:
'*My name is Ozymandias, king of kings;*
Look on my works, ye Mighty, and despair!'
Nothing beside remains. Round the decay
Of that colossal wreck, boundless and bare,
The lone and level sands stretch far away."'

So much for power and fame! Unlike that of poor old Ozymandias, whoever he was, the poetic fame of Shelley still endures.

Chapter Eleven

JOHN KEATS
1795–1821

A Fighting Poet

It's back to the working class for our next poet. Keats's father ran a livery stable, a place that hired out horses.

Keats was the eldest of four children; he had two brothers and a sister. He grew up – though not very far – and was sent to school in Enfield. He was a tough, cheerful lad, not all that keen on his studies. Despite his small size he was a lively scrapper. When he was nine his father died, killed by a fall from a horse. His mother remarried and her new husband immediately sold the stables. The newly-weds took off, and the children were sent off to live with their grandmother.

I'm no scrap- I'm a scrapper!'

A Mother Lost and Found – and Lost Again

A few years later, Keats's mother left her new husband and came back to the family. Keats was delighted – only to be cast down when two years later, she died of tuberculosis.

He took refuge in his studies reading widely, and winning prizes at school. He became friends with one of his tutors, Cowden Clarke, who introduced him to the pleasures of poetry. Soon Keats was starting to write poetry of his own.

It was time to think about earning a living. Keats, influenced perhaps by his mother's illness, decided on the medical profession. He was apprenticed to a doctor, and then went on to study at Guy's Hospital.

Apothecary or Poet?

But by now Keats was keener on poetry than on medicine. His friend Clarke introduced him to Leigh Hunt, a well-known poet, essayist and journalist. Hunt liked the poetry Keats showed him, and encouraged him to continue. (Hunt was a bit of a radical. He got into trouble for publishing a poem in which he called the Prince Regent a fatty. Perfectly true, but Hunt still got sent to prison – for two years! You didn't mess with the royals in those days.)

Keats passed his exams in 1816, qualifying as an apothecary and surgeon – and horrified his family by giving up medicine for poetry.

Early Works

He published his first volume in 1817. It was early stuff but it contained at least one promising, and later to be famous, poem 'On First Looking Into Chapman's Homer.'

Keats, not being a real gent, had never studied Latin and Greek. Chapman's translation made the Classical Greek poet accessible.

'Then felt I like some watcher of the skies
When a new planet swims into his ken;
Or like stout Cortez when with eagle eyes
He star'd at the Pacific – and all his men
Look'd at each other with a wild surmise
Silent, upon a peak in Darien.'

(Stout means 'stout-hearted' – not that Cortez, the explorer referred to, was a fatty like the Prince Regent.)

Keats Carries On

Keats lacked influential friends, and the snobbish critics of the day paid little attention to his poetry. Persevering, Keats wrote a long Elizabethan-style ballad called 'Endymion' about a shepherd who marries the goddess Diana.

It was published in 1818 and this time the critics did take notice – they tore it to shreds. Keats, who was known to be a friend of that well-known lefty, Leigh Hunt, was dismissed as a member of 'the Cockney school of poetry' and advised to stick to his pills and potions.

And On!

Still determined to make his name as a poet, Keats set off on a walking tour with a friend called Brown, through the Lakes, up to Scotland, and on to Ireland. Eventually he fell ill and had to come home. On his return, he set to work on another long poem called 'Hyperion'. But Fate had more setbacks in store. His brother Tom fell ill with tuberculosis. Keats, still none too well himself, looked after him until his brother died at the end of the year – catching the illness himself in the process.

Ill and in Love

By 1819 Keats's own health was failing. He moved to his friend Brown's house in Hampstead. There he met, and fell madly in love with, a beautiful young girl called Fanny Brawne.

Keats had very little money left by now. A scheme to write a money-making tragedy didn't work out. He wrote the play, 'Otho' but Drury Lane and Covent Garden refused to put it on.

Never Say Die

Keats refused to give up. He went on working on 'Hyperion' and started another long poem, 'Lamia'. He started a new play, and became secretly engaged to Fanny Brawne.

In 1820 Keats published his final volume of poetry – and got a good review – at last – from the prestigious 'Edinburgh Review', the publication that had clobbered Byron.

Keats's health was much worse now, and the doctors advised a milder climate. His publisher advanced some money, and he went off to Italy with a painter friend, Joseph Severn. He died in Rome in 1821. He was just over 25 years old.

A Brief Career

Keats's poetry-writing life covers just three years, from 1816 to 1819. In this short time he achieved an amazing amount. Besides his three long narrative poems, he wrote a number of odes and sonnets, many of them masterpieces.

'The Eve of St Agnes' is a medieval ballad, not unlike Coleridge's 'Christabel', set in the traditional castle.

'St Agnes Eve – ah, bitter chill it was,
The owl, for all his feathers, was a-cold
The hare limp'd trembling through the frozen grass
And silent were the sheep in woolly fold.'

The beautiful young maiden, Madeline, goes to bed, hoping for a magical vision of her lover. Little does she know that her boyfriend has smuggled himself into her room. There's definitely no naughtiness though. It's all very spiritual and high-flown, and the poem ends happily with an elopement:

'And they are gone: aye, ages long ago,
These lovers fled away into the storm . . .'

An Unlucky Knight

In 'La Belle Dame sans Merci' a wandering knight meets a beautiful magical lady, and gives her a ride on his horse. They go to her 'elfin grot' for a spot of hanky-panky:

'And there I shut her wild wild eyes
With kisses four.'

The knight falls asleep and has a nasty nightmare:

'I saw pale kings and princes too,
Pale warriors, death-pale were they all;
Who cried "La Belle Dame sans Merci
Hath thee in thrall."'

He wakes and finds himself alone 'on the cold hill's side' (these Essex girls are all the same). After that

'You shouldn't be out on a dirty Knight my love!'

he just hangs around, presumably in hope of another date.

'And that is why I sojourn here
Alone and palely loitering,
Though the sedge is withered from the lake,
And no birds sing.'

Some Other Odes

There's the famous 'Ode to Autumn':

'Season of mists and mellow fruitfulness . . .'

'... Seasons of mists and mellow fruitfulness... are causing delays to the 8·53 to Paddington!'

and the 'Ode to a Nightingale' and its immortal song:

'The same that oft-times hath
Charm'd magic casements, opening on the foam
Of perilous seas, in faery lands forlorn.'

Keats had many troubles in his short life, but it would be wrong to see him just as as a tragic figure. It's true he was sometimes oppressed with melancholy – and no wonder – but for much of the time he was a lively, cheerful character with a gift for friendship. Perhaps he's best remembered in the poem he wrote for his sister:

'There was a naughty boy
And a naughty boy was he
For nothing would he do
But scribble poetry . . .'

Keats wasn't properly appreciated in his lifetime, but his reputation grew after his death. With some poets it's the other way round . . .

Chapter Twelve

ALFRED, LORD TENNYSON
1809–1892

Victorian Values

We're coming to the Victorians now, serious men with serious whiskers, who wore suits, waistcoats and top hats. Most prominent of the Victorian poets is Alfred Tennyson. He had a stormy family history. Alfred's father, George Tennyson, had quarrelled violently with *his* father, and been disinherited in favour of his own younger brother. Not unnaturally, Alfred's dad got all bitter and twisted, and became a clergyman and a violent alcoholic. (Sunday sermons must have been fun!)

'There'll be no Holy Communion thish Shunday – we've run out of wine!'

Alfred Goes Up

Sixth of twelve children (you've got to admit it, they had stamina in those days), Alfred was keen on poetry from childhood. By the time

60

he went up to Cambridge in 1827 he'd already published over fifty poems in a volume called 'Poems by Two Brothers'. A serious-minded young man, Alfred did well at Cambridge, winning the Chancellor's Gold Medal for Poetry.

Alfred and Arthur

He also formed an intense friendship with a brilliant young man called Arthur Hallam. The two became best mates. They went on continental holidays together.

Alfred published another volume of poetry called, 'Poems, Chiefly Lyrical.' The literary hatchet-men of the time thought it should have been called, 'Poems, Chiefly Terrible' and they tore it to bits. Two of the poems at least are still remembered.

'Marianna' is all about a love-lorn lady in a moated grange:

'With blackest moss the flower
    plots
Were thickly crusted one and
    all
The rusted nails fell from
    the knots
That held the pear to the
    gable wall . . .'

The lady is waiting for her absent lover, presumably so he can do a bit of gardening. He doesn't turn up and she's really fed up:

'She only said, "My life is dreary,
He cometh not," she said.
She said, "I am aweary, aweary,
I would that I were dead!"'

'...and that coat of arms belonged to the Knight who loved Oriana'.

'Oriana' is a medieval-style ballad, about a knight, defeated in battle, crying out to his lost love:

'They should have slain me where I lay
Oriana!
I could not see the light of day
Oriana!'

(A later poet, Robert Graves suggested the poem would be much improved if you substituted 'Bottom upwards!' for 'Oriana!')

Tennyson's Troubles

In 1833, Tennyson's friend Arthur Hallam died suddenly and unexpectedly while abroad. Tennyson was shattered. Many years later, he published 'In Memoriam', a long poem in which he mourns the loss of his friend – 'the most perfect human being I have ever known'.

At about this time Tennyson's father died, and he had to leave university to help look after the family. He also became engaged. (The eager lovers didn't marry until nearly twenty years later.)

'That's one of Emily's Engagement Presents!'

Alfred Carries On

Somehow Tennyson managed to continue his work as a poet. His reputation was firmly established by the two-volume 'Poems', published in 1842. This included such poems as 'Ulysses', 'Morte D'Arthur', 'Sir Galahad', and his social protest poem, 'Locksley Hall'. Also in this collection was 'Break, Break, Break', inspired by the death of his friend Hallam:

'Break, break, break,
On thy cold grey stones, Oh Sea!
And I would that my tongue could utter
The thoughts that arise in me.'

Poet's Progress

In 1845 Tennyson was given a Civil List pension, the Arts Council Grant of the time, of £200 a year. Relieved of financial worries, Tennyson went on to have a long and distinguished career. In 1847 he published 'The Princess' advocating women's rights (now there's a mad idea for you!). In 1850 he succeeded Wordsworth as Poet Laureate, and finally married his patient fiancée. In 1859 he published the epic 'Idylls of the King', a series of long narrative poems about King Arthur and his knights. Shy and retiring by nature, Tennyson found himself an increasingly important public figure. In 1883 he was made a Baron, becoming Alfred, Lord Tennyson. He continued writing poetry for the rest of his long life and died, aged 83 in 1892, surpassing even Wordsworth as a Grand Old Man of English poetry.

The Good, the Bad and the Beautiful

Today the Arthurian epics and the long verse romances can be heavy going. But Tennyson was one of the finest poets of his age, and his massive output contains many wonderful works.

There's the unforgettable 'Charge of the Light Brigade' celebrating one of the most famous cock-ups in military history.

> '*Half a league, half a league*
> *Half a league onward,*
> *All in the valley of Death*
> *Rode the six hundred . . .*
> *"Forward the Light Brigade"*
> *Was there a man dismay'd?'*

(There were six hundred probably!) Still:

> '*Their's not to reason why,*
> *Their's but to do or die.'*

There are the noble sentiments of 'Lady Clara Vere de Vere':

'Kind hearts are more than coronets
And simple faith than Norman blood.'

A character in 'Locksley Hall' hates getting out of bed:

'Comrades, leave me here a little, while as yet 'tis early morn
Leave me here, and when you want me, sound upon the bugle horn'.

(I bet that shifted him!)

There's even a bit of science fiction style prophecy:

'For I dipt into the fortune, far as human eye could see,
Saw the Vision of the world, and all the wonder that would be.
Saw the heavens fill with commerce, argosies of magic sails,
Pilots of the purple twilight, dropping down with costly bales
Heard the heavens filled with shouting and there rained a ghastly dew.
From the nations' airy navies, grappling in the central blue'.

Air-freight traffic and the Battle of Britain – not bad for 1842! In a late poem, Tennyson looks peacefully ahead to his death, to slipping away from life like a sailing ship leaving harbour:

'Sunset and evening star
And one clear call for me
And let there be no moaning on the bar
When I put out to sea . . .'

Chapter Thirteen

ROBERT BROWNING
1812–1889

Bouncing Bob

Browning isn't one of your shy and sensitive poets. He was a sturdy type, full of life and energy – just like his poetry. He was a London lad, born in Camberwell, educated at Peckham School, and, briefly, at London University – he dropped out after six months. Luckily for Browning, he had the one thing every aspiring poet needs – a kind-hearted dad. His father was a mild-mannered, culturally-minded Bank of England clerk, with his own library of six thousand

'Father – you *even* have a first edition of "The Art of Fly fishing" by J. R. Hartley!'

books. He was happy to have a poet in the family, and quite willing to support him. Apart from trips abroad, also at Dad's expense, Robert lived at home until he was thirty-four.

Popular 'Paracelsus'

After travel in Russia and in Italy, Browning came up with the goods by producing 'Paracelsus', a long philosophical poem about the life of a sixteenth-century mystic. The poem was a critical hit, and Browning's career was launched. He started mixing with the literary set, and met famous writers of the time – like Tennyson and a promising young newcomer called Dickens.

Unsuccessful 'Sordello'

After several attempts at writing for the stage – his plays were all flops – Browning returned to poetry. Hoping to repeat the success of 'Paracelsus', he produced another long narrative poem, this time about the life of an Italian troubadour. Described as 'the development of a soul', the poem was written in a complex, condensed style. Today it's recognised as one of Browning's major works. At the time it was seen as long, complicated and confusing. The critics hated it. One claimed he'd only understood the first line of the immensely long poem:

'Who wills may hear Sordello's story told . . .'

– and the last:

'Who would has heard *Sordello's story told.'*

Everything in between had him completely baffled!

Browning Battles On

A feebler poet might have retired hurt, but Browning worked steadily on producing no less than eight books of verse over the next five years. These were shorter, more dramatic poems, written in a wide variety of forms and metres. One of them, 'Pippa Passes', includes one of Browning's best loved and most quoted lyrics:

'The year's at the spring
And day's at the morn;
Morning's at seven;
The hill-side's dew-pearled;
The lark's on the wing;
The snail's on the thorn:
God's in his heaven,
All's right with the world!'

'I see the snails on the thorn – it must be spring'

'Dramatic Lyrics' contains the spine-chilling 'My Last Duchess'. A proud and arrogant nobleman explains why he found it necessary to have his beautiful young wife murdered:

' . . . She had
A heart – how shall I say? – too soon made glad,
Too easily impressed; she liked whate'er
She looked on, and her looks went everywhere.'

There's no suggestion that she's unfaithful – he just can't stand the way she's as nice to everyone else as she is to *him*:

' . . . Oh, sir, she smiled, no doubt,
Whene'er I passed her; but who passed without
Much the same smile? This grew; I gave commands;
Then all smiles stopped together.'

The equally chilling 'Porphyria' tells how a jealous lover becomes convinced that, just for one precious moment, his unfaithful mistress really loves him. So, to preserve that precious moment, he kills her.

> '... All her hair
> In one long yellow string I wound
> Three times her little throat around
> And strangled her. No pain felt she;
> I am quite sure she felt no pain.'

Other poems include the famous 'Pied Piper of Hamelin':

> 'Anything like the sound of a rat
> Makes my heart go pit-a-pat!'

'He's quite good, but I prefer Tina Turner!'

There's the rollicking 'How they Brought the Good News from Ghent to Aix':

> 'I sprang to the stirrup, and Joris, and he
> I galloped, Dirck galloped, we galloped all three.'

No-one seems to know what the good news was, who was bringing it to whom, or why. Who cares? It was obviously a hell of a ride!

A Poet's Comeback

A steady flow of fine poems soon restored Browning's reputation. The dramatic instincts that had failed on the stage found full expression in his poetry. Eventually Browning had another go at the epic, successfully this time. 'The Ring and the Book' is an immensely long narrative poem. It tells, through a number of vividly-described characters, the true story of a historical Italian murder trial, and its success made Browning famous. Eventually, like Wordsworth and Tennyson before him, he became one of English Literature's Grand Old Men.

Robert Browning died, aged 77, in Venice in his beloved Italy. He is buried in Westminster Abbey, in Poets' Corner.

Love Story

Browning will always be remembered for his romance with Elizabeth Barrett – it's one of Eng Lit's great love stories. Returning from one of his visits to Italy, Browning read the newly published volume of Elizabeth's poems, and was so impressed that he wrote to the author. A correspondence followed, and eventually a series of meetings. The two poets fell madly in love. But there were problems. Elizabeth's health was bad. It was feared than any kind of excitement or exertion might kill her off. Mr Barrett, Elizabeth's tyrannical and possessive father, wouldn't hear of her getting married.

A Happy Ending

A lesser man might have given up – but not Robert Browning. Since there was no hope of Mr Barrett's permission, he decided to do without it. Overcoming all Elizabeth's fears and worries, he swept her off her feet, probably literally, and they eloped together. After a secret marriage, he carried her off to Italy, and they settled in Florence.

'Come back Elizabeth – pizzas will be bad for your health !'

Free of the stifling atmosphere of her family, Elizabeth's health miraculously improved. She spent the rest of her life as a lively and active wife and mother. After fifteen years of blissfully happy marriage, she died in Browning's arms.

69

Some of her finest poetry is a celebration of their love.

> *'How do I love thee? Let me count the ways . . .*
> *I love thee to the depth and breadth and height*
> *My soul can reach,'*

'You've now counted twelve million different ways of loving me
— please leave off Elizabeth!'

she writes in 'Sonnets from the Portuguese':

> *'Smiles, tears of all my life! And if God choose,*
> *I shall but love thee better after death.'*

70

Chapter Fourteen

CHARLES DICKENS
1812–1870

The Inimitable

We come now to another of Eng Lit's superstars – Charles Dickens, or, as he was known at the time – 'The Inimitable!'

Dickens's father, John Dickens, was a clerk in the Navy pay office. An amiable, easy-going type, he was quite incapable of staying out of debt, and eventually finished up in prison. His family, as was the custom in those days, moved into prison to live with him. All except for young Charles, by then twelve years old. He was put into cheap lodgings and sent to work at Warren's Blacking Warehouse, sticking labels on bottles. He was only there for a few months but he felt he'd been abandoned, 'thrown away' as he put it. The experience marked him for life.

A lucky legacy got John Dickens out of prison, and Dickens was able to go back to school. He grew up into a lively, handsome, intelligent young man, fizzing with energy and fiercely determined to succeed. He became a solicitor's clerk, but soon tired of the slow-moving life of the law. Teaching himself shorthand, he got a job as a parliamentary reporter, reporting members' speeches from the reporters' gallery in the House of Commons, and from political meetings all over the country. He began to see something of London life, developed a passion for the theatre – and fell madly in love.

Dickens in Love

Maria Beadnell was the daughter of a bank manager. She was beautiful but fickle, with many other admirers. Continually blowing hot and cold, she gave poor Dickens a hard time. Her parents

weren't keen on their daughter marrying a penniless young nobody, so they broke up the affair by sending Maria abroad.

Young Dickens was heartbroken – and Maria's parents had made an all-time bad decision. A few years later, their daughter's penniless boyfriend was rich and famous.

Dickens had been writing comic pieces for magazines, under the pen-name 'Boz'. Eventually they were collected in a book, 'Sketches by Boz'. Some publishers came to the young writer with a proposition. They'd commission a series of comic drawings, and Dickens could write some comic text to go with them . . .

Mr Pickwick

Dickens grabbed hold of the scheme and made it his own. To use his words, 'I thought of Mr Pickwick . . .'

'Pickwick Papers', as the book was to be called, is the story of the wanderings of Mr Pickwick, a kindly, well-heeled old codger who wanders round the countryside getting into trouble, perpetually being conned by the fast-talking Mr Jingle. It was published in monthly instalments – Dickens was to stay with this method of publication all his life. 'Pickwick' sold slowly at first, but with the invention of Sam Weller, Mr Pickwick's comic Cockney servant, it suddenly took off. Soon people were queueing up to buy the instalments as they appeared. 'Pickwick' became a bestseller and Dickens, still only twenty-four, was on his way. He could even afford a wife. He married Catherine Hogarth, the daughter of a fellow journalist.

A Busy Life

Dickens followed 'Pickwick' with the even more popular 'Oliver Twist', the famous story of the orphan boy who 'asked for more'. Over the years, he wrote twelve more novels, many of them bestsellers. He became a celebrity, well-known in fashionable society, and for his work for a number of good causes – like the establishment of a home for 'fallen women'. He travelled on the Continent and in America, and he edited magazines like 'Household Words'. Keen as ever on the theatre, he organised numerous amateur productions, once even performing before Queen Victoria.

A Theatrical Affair

He'd been married to Catherine for over twenty years by now and they had ten children. But the marriage had never been a real success. Dickens had chosen Catherine because she was calm and easy-going, unlike his first love, the wilful and spoiled Maria Beadnell. Unfortunately, poor Catherine was so placid that she drove the restless and often-irritable Dickens crazy. He often treated her unkindly and over the years they grew steadily further apart. Then in the course of one of his amateur productions Dickens fell romantically in love with a young actress called Ellen Ternan. Eventually Catherine and Dickens separated. The affair doesn't seem to have brought anyone much happiness. Dickens didn't really have the temperament for this sort of thing, and he felt guilty about Catherine. Ellen, a respectable girl at heart, was unhappy in an illicit relationship.

Dickens on Stage

In his later years, Dickens turned to an extraordinary venture – he began to give public readings. They were a smash-hit. The public flocked to hear the great man and Dickens gave them good value, performing rather than reading. When he enacted the murder of Nancy by Bill Sikes from 'Oliver Twist', the effect was so terrifying

that nervous ladies were frequently known to faint . . . The readings were extraordinarily profitable, especially those in America. Dickens loved performing, even though the strain of the performances was beginning to affect his health. Despite the pleas of his friends, and the warnings of his doctor, Dickens insisted on carrying on. In 1870 he collapsed during one of the performances, and died soon afterwards. He was buried in Westminster Abbey, amidst scenes of nationwide mourning.

The Man and the Work

Dickens wrote fourteen novels in all. Crammed with plots and sub-plots, packed with wonderful characters, they cover a variety of

'Your fiancée might've got delayed by British Rail Miss Havisham!'

themes. Many deal with the social evils of the day, and much is made of Dickens as a novelist of social reform. But although he was a warm-hearted man with a real sympathy for the sufferings of the poor – after all, he'd known hard times himself – he never had any very clear ideas about how to improve things. His only thought was that the rich people should be more like Mr Pickwick, kind and generous to the poor people . . . Dickens's real concerns are usually personal and emotional.

'Oliver Twist' attacks the cruel 'workhouse' system – but it also reflects the loneliness and abandonment Dickens felt in his childhood. Little Orphan Oliver may be a bit too good to be true, but there's the wonderfully evil Fagin and the terrifying Sikes to make up for it. Not to mention the Artful Dodger, and the immortal Mr Bumble the Beadle with his much-quoted observation that 'The law is a ass!'

'Don't bother with silk hankies boys – go for their credit cards!'

'Nicholas Nickleby' was written to expose the notorious 'Yorkshire Schools' where unwanted children were packed off just to get rid of them. The headmaster, Wackford Squeers, has his own version of the national curriculum.

'C-l-e-a-n, clean, verb active, to make bright, to scour. W-i-n, win, d-e-r, der, winder, a casement. When the boy knows this out of the book he goes and does it.'

Little David, Little Dorrit and Little Nell

'David Copperfield', the novel Dickens called his 'favourite child', has many parallels with his own life. The feckless Mr Micawber, always waiting for 'something to turn up', is a portrait of Dickens's father.

Mr Micawber, incidentally, gives the best financial advice ever:

'Annual income twenty pounds, annual expenditure nineteen, nineteen, six, result happiness. Annual income twenty pounds, annual expenditure twenty pounds nought and six, result misery.'

Pity he could never manage to follow it!

Little David is sent off to work in a wine warehouse, very like Dickens's dreaded Blacking Warehouse. Like Dickens, David becomes a famous writer. Unlike Dickens, he finally finds happiness with his one true love.

'Little Dorrit' explores repressive Christianity, Civil Service delays, and the effects of long imprisonment.

'The Old Curiosity Shop' gives us one of the most loved, or loathed, characters in fiction, the saintly Little Nell, who tries to look after her gambling-mad grandpa while persecuted by the evil dwarf Quilp. Her tragic death had the whole country in tears – except for Oscar Wilde, who said, 'It requires a heart of stone not to laugh . . .'

Law and Disorder

'Bleak House' deals with the Law's delays, 'Barnaby Rudge' and 'A Tale of Two Cities' with the horrors of revolution, 'Hard Times' with the evil effects of unfeeling industrialisation. 'Dombey and Son' is the story of a proud and haughty man who ignores his loving daughter. He treasures his beautiful wife, his prosperous business, and the little son who will one day be his heir – and has only his daughter to turn to when he loses all three. In 'Great Expectations' Dickens tackles the problems of a sudden change from poverty to wealth, and the question of what really makes a gentleman. 'Our Mutual Friend' also deals with the destructive effects of riches, as does the now-forgotten 'Martin Chuzzlewit'.

Dickens's last book, 'Edwin Drood', is a detective story about drugs and murder in a cathedral town. Sadly, he died before it was finished, so we can never be absolutely sure whodunit – though there are plenty of theories . . .

'I gave up coming to bed with great expectations years ago!'

An Excess of Success

Enormously popular in his own lifetime, Dickens was later to be undervalued because of his own success. Snobbish critics dismissed him as a popular entertainer, a crowd-pleasing creator of comic characters. Today however, the poetic power of his writing, especially in the later, darker novels, and the amazing variety of his talent are beginning to be appreciated once more. Just as with Shakespeare, you get the feeling of enormous energy coupled with boundless, overflowing talent.

Today, like the Victorians, we can appreciate Charles Dickens for what he really is – The Inimitable!

Chapter Fifteen

THE UNBELIEVABLE BRONTËS

Charlotte Brontë – 1816–1855

We come now to the most amazing family in Eng Lit – three sisters and a brother. Between them they produced two geniuses, sorry, genii, one very good writer and one drunk.

Charlotte, Emily and Anne Brontë were the children of the Reverend Patrick Brontë, an Irish-born minister, who'd finished up at Haworth in Yorkshire. The children's mother died when they were young. The three sisters and their brother, Branwell, grew up together in the lonely parsonage on the Yorkshire Moors.

It was Branwell, of course, who was the bright hope of the family. Branwell himself was quite convinced he was a genius. He had only one problem – he just couldn't make his mind up whether to be a great writer or a famous artist. The three sisters were there to be his fan club. After all, they were only girls . . .

A Box of Soldiers

One day dad brought home a box of wooden soldiers. The three girls seized on them, and used them to create imaginary kingdoms with names like Angria and Gondal. They wrote pages and pages . . .

'We've been posted to Angria and Gondal!'

'Where the Hell's that?'

Jobs for the Girls

The Reverend Patrick was far from well off, and the girls had to make some attempt to earn their own livings.

Charlotte became a governess, a private teacher for the children of well-off families. She held a couple of posts as a governess, though she didn't care for it too much. Fiercely independent, she resented her lowly position. Then she and her sister, Emily, went off to Brussels to study languages at the Maison d'Education. Charlotte promptly fell in love with her teacher. But the Professor wasn't interested. He ignored her soulful glances, and refused to answer her notes. (He was the headmistress's husband, so he may have been worried about job-security.)

Back home in Yorkshire, Branwell was still getting ready to amaze the world. To pass the time, all three sisters started scribbling novels.

'Between the 3 of us, we've destroyed quite a bit of rain forest!'

Charlotte's was based on her unhappy love affair in Brussels – only in the book it was the teacher who fell for *her*! Charlotte's novel, 'The Professor' was turned down. But Anne's and Emily's were accepted!

Charlotte's Masterpiece

Charlotte tried again, and in 1847 she came up with a masterpiece. 'Jane Eyre' is the original blueprint for the Gothic Romantic Novel. The heroine, small and plain and a humble governess – like Charlotte – takes a post in the lonely old house of the hero – or is he the villain? Aha! Mr Rochester is a fierce, ruthless character with a murky past. She falls madly in love with him, he ignores her or treats her with scorn. There are mysterious goings-on and strange noises in the night. Mr Rochester is romantically involved with a rich society beauty. Our heroine can only look on and suffer. *But* – this is the unlikely bit – the hero-villain comes to realise it's the plain little governess he really loves. He proposes, she accepts. Then, up pops his dark past – in the shape of a mad wife locked up in the attic. More misery for our heroine who goes off in despair. Luckily, if that's the word, the mad wife burns the house down, conveniently dying in the flames. Rochester is blinded in the blaze. Re-enter our faithful heroine. In the immortal words of the novel:

'*Reader, I married him.*'

Success and Tragedy

'Jane Eyre' was published that same year. It was a scandalous success. But although the Brontës were talented, they were short on staying power. By the time Charlotte's second novel, a historical tale called 'Shirley', was finished, her sisters and brother were dead. She wrote a third novel, 'Villette', another rewrite of her Brussels love story, and married her father's curate – despite the opposition of her father, who refused to come to the wedding. A year later she died of a severe chill – all that wandering on the windy moors. (Her rejected first novel, 'The Professor', was published after her death.)

Emily's Story 1818–1848

Altogether wilder and more passionate than her sister, Emily too loved nothing better than to roam the windswept lonely moors. Her one and only book, 'Wuthering Heights', reflects her stormy temperament. Violent, dramatic, filled with a brooding sense of the supernatural, it tells of the doomed and death-wish-ridden romance of the heroine Cathy and the demonic Heathcliffe. 'Wuthering Heights' is an astonishing work, mad, melodramatic and way over the top. Emily's sister Charlotte said it was filled with 'a horror of great darkness.' Today 'Wuthering Heights' is seen as a work of genius. But, unlike 'Jane Eyre', it wasn't well received at the time.

'Emily's writing another stormy bit in Wuthering Heights, father!'

The reviews were terrible, and Emily abandoned her second novel. She caught a chill at her brother Branwell's funeral and died a few months later.

Sister Anne 1820–1849

Anne was the youngest of the three sisters. Like Charlotte she became a governess, and her first novel 'Agnes Grey' tells of the trials of a governess's life. In 1845 Anne was working in the same household as her brother Branwell, who was employed as a tutor. Branwell was caught carrying-on with the lady of the house. He was swiftly given the boot – and Anne with him. She got her own back

'LOOK on the bright side sis, I get caught with the Mistress, we both get sacked – it makes a great story!'

though. Her second novel, 'The Tenant of Wildfell Hall', tells of the degeneration of an alcoholic – and it was based directly on her study of Branwell. With its savage exposure of a drunken and abusive husband, 'The Tenant of Wildfell Hall' has been recently re-discovered by the feminists. Still only twenty-nine, Anne died of consumption, on a holiday trip to Scarborough. Like her sisters, she was a martyr to howling gales on the moors and icy draughts indoors. If only they'd invented central heating.

Brother Branwell 1817–1848

Branwell started out with the highest hopes – and finished up as the black sheep of the family. Somehow his promised career in Art and Literature never got off the ground. Meanwhile, his amazingly talented sisters were quietly scribbling away, edging him out of the limelight. Mind you, he took his disappointment like a man – he promptly turned to opium and booze. (He'd have got on well with old Coleridge.) Branwell ended up as an assistant clerk on the railway, but he soon got the sack for negligence. After that he went into a decline and died. Poor old Branwell – overshadowed by his three famous sisters, he's condemned to be a mere footnote in English Literature . . .

'Three famous sisters and all I ever wrote was a British Rail Time Table – of course I'm depressed!'

Chapter Sixteen

GEORGE ELIOT
1819–1880

A Girl Called George

Back in the nineteenth century, writing novels wasn't really a respectable occupation for 'the fair sex'. Jane Austen published her first book anonymously. The Brontë sisters used the unlikely masculine pen-names of Currer, Ellis and Acton Bell. Mary Ann Evans called herself George Eliot. She was what the Victorians called a 'blue-stocking' – a well-educated, independently-minded young woman who considered herself the equal of any man.

Mary Ann, or Marian as she liked to be called, was the daughter of an estate manager. She was very bright, but unfortunately far from beautiful. Unkind people said she looked rather like a horse with ringlets. The novelist Henry James said she was 'magnificently ugly – deliciously hideous!'

Marian did well at school, and worked even harder after she left, studying Italian, Greek, Latin, German and French. She eventually became assistant editor of the Westminster Review, a high-powered intellectual periodical.

Five languages is a lot of horse sense

A Sacred Bond

Her new job brought her into contact with writers of the day, like Tennyson and Dickens. Amongst them was an actor, dramatist and essayist called George Henry Lewes. George was clearly a man who valued brains and character more than mere beauty – or maybe he was just very fond of horses. Anyway, George and Marian fell in love. They were unable to marry, because George was married already. Even though his wife had deserted him for another man,

George couldn't get a divorce because he'd 'condoned' or agreed to the adultery. George and Marian came to a very bold decision. They decided to ignore public opinion and to go ahead and live openly together as man and wife – something that just wasn't done in those days. They were happy together for over twenty years. At first they were social outcasts, but in time people got used

George meets George

to the idea. As Marian herself put it: 'Our marriage is not a legal one, though it is regarded by us both as a sacred bond.'

Marian's Career

George encouraged Marian to try her hand at fiction. She wrote under the name of 'George Eliot' – 'George' because it was George

I encourage Marian to write, as long as she doesn't neglect her household duties!

Lewes's name, 'Eliot' because it had a good, solid sound. She used a man's name because she felt the public was less likely to buy and read books written by a woman – particularly a woman who was living in an 'immoral' relationship.

Unhappy Hetty

In 1859 she published 'Adam Bede', the story of a farmer's daughter, Hetty Sorel, who is loved by the noble carpenter of the title but seduced by the wicked squire. (Where would the novel be without its wicked squires?) Hetty gets pregnant, is abandoned, and her baby dies. Hetty ends up condemned to death for infanticide, though the sentence is reduced to transportation to Australia. Strong stuff for its day, 'Adam Bede' was a great success. People started to wonder who the author really was . . .

'Trouble at the Mill'

George Eliot's next book, 'The Mill on the Floss', is the tangled tale of Tom and Maggie Tulliver, the miller's two children. Wild and rebellious Maggie falls for sensitive, crippled Phillip, son of the local lawyer. A feud develops between miller and lawyer, and Tom forbids Maggie to see Phillip again. Maggie visits her cousin Lucy, gets compromised by Lucy's fiancé Stephen, turned out by brother Tom, and ostracised by the village. Everything ends unhappily with a huge flood. Tom and Maggie make up – just before they drown in each other's arms! 'Mill on the Floss' got rather a mixed reception. George Eliot's real identity had leaked out by now, and there was quite a scandal.

Successful Silas

However Marian's next book, 'Silas Marner', was a smash hit. Silas is a weaver, made bitter and twisted by a false accusation of theft. He becomes a solitary miser, slowly building up a little hoard of gold – which gets nicked by the squire's wicked son Dunstan – clearly no relation to the well-known saint. Silas is shattered, but slowly finds consolation and happiness in caring for Eppie, the unwanted child of his brother Godfrey. 'Silas Marner' was followed by 'Romola', a historical tale. It was pretty much a failure – and Marian's next novel 'Felix Holt' was actually rejected by the publishers.

The accursed Vatman must have called when I was out! \

Masterly Middlemarch

Undeterred, Marian carried on writing. In 1871 she came out with 'Middlemarch', her acknowledged masterpiece. A long and complicated saga – it was first published in *eight* volumes – 'Middlemarch' combines a number of plot-strands. Idealistic young Dorothea marries dry-as-dust old scholar Doctor Casaubon, because she admires his mind. It doesn't work out (surprise surprise!). She falls for his handsome young cousin Will. Other characters include Fred and Rosamund, son and daughter of the mayor of Middlemarch. Dad wants cheerful and easy-going Fred to be a clergyman. Fred's fiancé Mary won't marry him unless he gives up the idea and settles down. Sister Rosamund, spoiled and wilful, captures the local doctor, Tertius Lydgate. Ignoring his serious ambitions, she pushes him into becoming a fashionable society doctor. They have a thoroughly unhappy married life, and he dies frustrated and worn out. Miserable old Casaubon kicks the bucket as well, and after various misunderstandings, Dorothea eventually marries her Will – though Casaubon has left a clause in *his* will – if she does she loses all his money . . .

' "Middlemarch" indeed – you've been reading it since the middle of October !'

'Middlemarch' was a massive success, making Marian not only famous but relatively rich. Dickens had just died, and she was now the leading novelist of the day.

Marian Gets Married

Her final work was less successful. 'Daniel Deronda' is the story of haughty Gwendolyn Harleth. She makes a loveless marriage for money, is thoroughly miserable, and becomes increasingly involved with Daniel Deronda, an idealistic young Jew.

'I'm a 'meliorist' John – and this isn't making life any better!'

Marian's faithful companion George Lewes died in 1878. Two years later, Marian achieved respect- ability again, by marrying John Cross, her accountant. (The mar- riage got off to rather a bad start. On their honeymoon in Venice, the bridegroom attempted suicide by jumping into the canal . . .) A few months later, Marian herself was dead. Despite her fame, they wouldn't have her in Westminster Abbey, and she was buried in Highgate Cemetery.

Marian's Mission

Before George Eliot, the novel had been seen largely as something rather frivolous, meant simply to entertain. A serious-minded, not to say solemn writer, Marian put a stop to all that. She saw herself, like the poet Wordsworth before her, as a teacher, a prophet and a sage. Her purpose was not just to entertain, but to instruct, to inform and to improve. Marian herself said she was a 'meliorist'. She believed it was possible for all of us to make life better by our own efforts – and you can't argue with that.

Chapter Seventeen

MARK TWAIN
1835–1910

Mississippi Sam

We haven't heard much from the Americans so far – perhaps they were too busy taming the Wild West. It's hard to find time for poetry and novels when you're fighting off the Apache, or driving a railroad through the Rocky Mountains. Early on, there was Fenimore Cooper with stirring stories of frontier life, like 'The Last of the Mohicans'. Later there were more refined types – like Henry James, who came to live in England, and became more English than the

'The West just ain't as wild as it used to be!'

English. One of the first native American writers to make a name in his own right was an unlikely character called Mark Twain. His real name was Samuel Langhorne Clemens, and he grew up in Hannibal on the Mississippi, the river with which he will always be associated. He was a Mississippi river-boat pilot for a time – and took his writing name from the pilots' cry as they sounded the depths of the shallow river: 'By the mark, twain!' (Twain meaning two fathoms.)

'Scraping bottom'

'You're quite right – Mark Twain wasn't Pilot on that particular boat!'

Sam in San Francisco

After serving in the Civil War, Twain spent some time roaming around the west, and prospected for silver in Nevada. He ended up working as a journalist in San Francisco. He wrote a comic short story, based on his experiences in the mining camps out west, called 'The Celebrated Jumping Frog of Calaveras County' – about a famous jumping frog that gets nobbled when someone feeds it

pellets of buckshot. Travel in Europe gave him material for 'Innocents Abroad'. Twain was a colourful character, a natural comedian, a witty and accomplished public speaker. Soon he was giving successful lecture tours both in America and in England. But his memories of his Mississippi childhood brought him true immortality.

Enter Tom Sawyer

In 1876 Mark Twain published 'The Adventures of Tom Sawyer'. Young Tom lives with his Aunt Polly in a quiet little town on the Mississippi. A lively, mischievous boy, Tom is usually in trouble. In one of the book's most famous sequences, he's ordered to whitewash the garden fence. As various friends come by, Tom convinces each one that whitewashing fences is the greatest fun in the world. He 'allows' each friend to paint a section of fence for him – at a price.

Tom's usual companion is the disreputable Huckleberry Finn. Together, Tom and Huck have a variety of amazing adventures, including saving the town drunk, falsely accused of murder, catching the real criminal and finding buried treasure. Mistakenly believed to be dead, they cause uproar by making a dramatic appearance at their own funeral service.

A Successful Sequel – Huckleberrry Finn

Huck tells his story in his own dry and homely style. Now independently wealthy, thanks to the discovery of buried treasure, he's been adopted by the kindly Widow Douglas who tries to educate him. She makes him read 'Pilgrim's Progress'.

'The statements,' says Huck, *'was interesting but tough.'*

Huck's villainous dad kidnaps him, in an attempt to get his hands on Huck's share of the treasure. Huck escapes and joins forces with Jim, a runaway slave. Huck and Jim decide to travel down the river by raft. They encounter all kinds of dangers, including feuding hillbillies and murderous mobs. Huck deals with them all in his own inimitable style.

'When you think about it – we lead a pretty humdrum existence!'

'Hain't we got all the fools in town on our side?' he says at one point. *'And ain't that a big enough majority in any town?'*

Huck Takes Off

Betrayed by a couple of callous con men, Jim is recaptured. Tom Sawyer turns up to help, and he and Huck manage to rescue Jim. Then Tom reveals that Jim has been free all along – his late mistress left him his freedom in her will. Aunt Polly turns up to sort things

'As a lad – I was very influenced by Huckleberry Finn!'

out and everything ends happily. Huck is due to be adopted by Tom's Aunt Sally.

'I reckon I got to light out for the territory,' says Huck. *'Aunt Sally. She's going to adopt me and civilise me and I can't stand it.'*

The book's off-hand, satirical account of the savagery of frontier life and the way it shows, without preaching, the evils of slavery, give 'Huckleberry Finn' more depth than 'Tom Sawyer'. Unusually for a sequel, the second book is reckoned to be even better than the first.

Doctor Twain

Twain was never to equal his success with Tom and Huck, though his historical novel 'The Prince and the Pauper' is still remembered. His view of the world seemed to darken in later life – there's a strain of deep pessimism in 'A Conecticut Yankee in King Arthur's Court' and 'Pudd'nhead Wilson'.

Mark Twain carried on writing and lecturing till the end of his long life. He was particularly proud of the Honorary Doctorate awarded to him by Oxford University in 1907 – not bad for a wandering westerner who left school when he was twelve! Twain died in 1910 – though a premature report of his death had appeared in the American press some time earlier. Twain, who was alive and well and touring Europe at the time, cabled back drily: 'The report of my death was an exaggeration . . .'

Chapter Eighteen

THOMAS HARDY
1840–1928

A Truly Rural Writer

It's back to the Brits now with our champion novelist of country life. Hardy wrote what are sometimes called pastoral novels. 'Pastoral' refers to the idea, very common amongst intellectual townies, that life is somehow nobler, purer and more beautiful in the country. (As long as you watch where you put your feet.)

Thomas Hardy, however, started out as a genuine countryman. He was born in Dorset, the son of a master stonemason and a serving-maid, educated at a local school, then apprenticed to a church architect in Dorchester. In 1862 he got a job in an architect's office in London where he spent his spare time visiting theatres and art galleries and trying to write poetry. Ill health forced him to go back to Dorchester, but he went on trying to write, moving on from poetry to novels.

I think I prefer writing stories to building storeys!

He also fell in love with his cousin, a sixteen-year-old girl called Tryphena Sparks. She in turn was involved with a close friend of Hardy's called Horace Moule, who later committed suicide at Cambridge. (Moule's suicide helped to form Hardy's often-gloomy view of life. He'd had a morbid streak from early youth. As a young man, he used to go and watch public executions in Dorchester.)

Tom Gets Going

Hardy's attempts at writing started to meet with success and he wrote a number of novels. He started off with a melodrama, 'Desperate Remedies' and followed it with a rustic comedy, 'Under the Greenwood Tree' and a rural romance, 'A Pair of Blue Eyes'. He was sent to work as an architect at St Juliot, Cornwall, where he met, fell in love with, and eventually married, the rector's sister-in-law, Emma Gifford. In 1874, the year of his marriage to Emma, he published his first major work, 'Far from the Madding Crowd'.

Beautiful Bathsheba

The novel is set in 'Wessex', an old name for the south-west of England which Hardy revived. It's the story of the proud and passionate beauty, Bathsheba Everdene, an independent-minded girl who actually runs her own farm. She is loved by a shepherd, the loyal and reliable Gabriel Oak, and wooed by a neighbouring farmer, Boldwood, and by the flashy Sergeant Troy, who is also busy

'I don't think having a soldier on the farm is going to work out!'

seducing one of her servants, Fanny Robin. Inevitably, Bathsheba makes the wrong choice and marries Troy, who treats her badly. The abandoned Fanny dies in childbirth, and Troy, stricken with remorse, disappears. Farmer Boldwood gives a party and proposes to Bathsheba, who says she'll marry him some day. Troy turns up, Boldwood goes mad and shoots him, and Bathsheba ends up with the faithful Gabriel, the only one left.

'Far from the Madding Crowd', at first published anonymously, was a huge success. It was considered to be so good that lots of people thought it must be by George Eliot!

High Output Hardy

When the truth came out, Hardy was launched as a full-time author. He packed in being an architect and went on to write twelve more novels, a number of short stories and a great many poems.

Among the best remembered of the novels are 'The Return of the Native', 'The Mayor of Casterbridge', and 'The Woodlanders'.

Tragic Tess

Perhaps the most famous of all Hardy's works is 'Tess of the D'Urbervilles', a steamy drama of country life. Tess Durbeyfield, a poor country girl, is distantly related to the noble family of the D'Urbervilles. She is seduced by the wicked Alec, who also claims to be a D'Urberville, and bears him a child which dies. Later, Tess seems about to find happiness and respectability when she marries Angel Clare, the son of a clergyman. On their wedding night she confesses her past sins (always a bad move) and the outraged Angel, no saint himself, throws her out and goes off to Brazil. The evil Alec re-appears and Tess, driven by poverty and desperation, becomes his mistress. Angel Clare comes back from Brazil, ready to forgive her, finds her living with Alec and clears off in a

'You look depressed dear, are you reading Thomas Hardy again?'

huff. Tess now feels Alec has ruined her life not once but twice, so when he comes home she stabs him. Tess finds a little happiness re-united with Angel Clare when they go into hiding together in the New Forest. Then she is arrested at Stonehenge, condemned to death, and hanged.

Tom in Trouble

Contemporary critics found the tale distressing and unpleasant and Hardy was accused of being pessimistic and immoral. However, the fuss about Tess was nothing to the storm of protest set off by what was to be Hardy's last novel, 'Jude the Obscure'.

Jude Makes It Bad

Jude is an intellectually-minded stonemason, trapped into marriage by the fickle Arabella. When she deserts him, leaving him to look after their son, Jude meets and falls in love with his neurotic cousin Sue, who rejects him for a schoolmaster. (Well, I said she was neurotic!) Once they are married, Sue finds she can't stand her schoolmaster, and runs back to Jude who takes her in. They live together and eventually have two children. However, they are outcasts, and desperately poor. When Sue announces that another child is on the way, the eldest child, son of Jude and Arabella, kills the two younger kids and commits suicide himself. Sue goes back to her schoolmaster. Jude goes on the bottle, ends up with Arabella and dies in misery.

(I wonder if he'd have felt any better if he'd realised the Beatles were going to write a song about him?)

More Brickbats for Tom

At the time, the publication of this cheery tale caused a storm of protest. 'The Pall Mall Gazette' called it 'dirt, drivel and damnation!' Hardy later recounted how the book was 'Burnt by a Bishop – probably in despair at not being able to burn me!' Anyway, Hardy took the hint, and gave up novels for poetry, which he'd always considered the superior form.

Back to Poetry

Hardy's future work included an immensely-long verse drama called 'The Dynasts', and a great deal of poetry, such as his volume of 'Wessex Poems.' 'The Dynasts' is concerned with the vast sweep of

'Is that the book of the soap opera I never liked on TV?'

history. Much of Hardy's poetry however concerns the simple pleasures, and sorrows, of country life:

> 'This is the weather the cuckoo likes,
> And so do I;
> When showers betumble the chestnut spikes,
> And nestlings fly;
> And the little brown nightingale bills his best,
> And they sit outside at the Traveller's Rest . . .'

Poet or Peasant?

In later life, Hardy's wife Emma began to turn peculiar. She was obsessed with her husband's social inferiority, and started referring to him as a peasant – a bit much when you think how much he'd achieved from fairly humble beginnings.

Emma died in 1912 and although they'd been drifting apart for years, Hardy was filled with grief, and wrote a number of poems about her. Two years later, he married his housekeeper and secretary, Florence Dugdale, living happily with her for the rest of his life.

Heart in the Country

In time the scandal about 'Jude' died down. Recognised as a fine poet and a major novelist, Hardy ended his life as another Grand Old Man of Eng Lit, showered with honours and honorary degrees. When he died, eighty-eight years old, in 1928, he was buried in Westminster Abbey. At least, most of him was. His heart was buried separately in a peaceful Wessex country churchyard. Thomas Hardy was always a country boy at heart . . .

'Please Sir, was Thomas Hardy the very first heart transplant?'

Chapter Nineteen

ROBERT LOUIS STEVENSON
1850–1894

Bloodthirsty Bob

Robert Louis Stevenson – RLS for short – was born in Edinburgh, the son of a lighthouse engineer. He inherited a bronchial condition

'One day son, All this could be yours!'

from his mother, and as a kid he was hardly allowed out, in case the fierce Scottish weather polished him off. His education was often interrupted by bouts of illness. Yet this sickly lad grew up to be an adventurous traveller, and to write some of the most bloodthirsty adventure stories in Eng Lit.

Student Days

Dad wanted him to follow family tradition, but Stevenson didn't fancy life on a lighthouse – he wanted to be a writer. They compromised – Stevenson studied law, so that at least he'd have a proper profession to fall back on.

Apparently RLS was a bit of a lad at Edinburgh University, dressing extravagantly, hitting the bottle, and mingling with Edinburgh lowlifes. (Perfectly normal student behaviour really.) This, together with Stevenson's developing doubts about Christianity, caused quite a few problems with his upright Victorian dad. Stevenson qualified as an advocate – that's Scottish for barrister – in 1875, but never used his degree. Instead he set off with a friend to journey through the canals of France by canoe – a pretty adventurous thing to do in those days. He later wrote an account of the trip called 'An Inland Voyage'. A later holiday, this time on a donkey, produced another travel book called, not surprisingly, 'Travels with a Donkey in the Cevennes'.

'They couldn't get the author, but they managed to get the donkey!'

RLS in Love

While he was in France, Stevenson met and fell madly in love with an American lady called Fanny Osbourne. She was ten years older than he was and married with two children. When she went back to America the holiday romance seemed to be over – but RLS wasn't a man to give up. Despite his still-dodgy health, he followed her all the way to San Francisco, travelling rough by emigrant ship and train, and persuaded her to divorce her

'I've travelled all the way from England to find you Fanny'

husband and marry him. He got another book out of the trip, of course – 'The Amateur Emigrant'. They spent their honeymoon in a disused silver mine. Stevenson got a book out of that too, 'The Silverado Squatters'. Poor Fanny – nevertheless she stayed devoted to him doing her best to nurse him back to health.

Treasure Island

Back home with his bride, RLS went to Scotland and in 1881 set to work on his first proper book. First serialised in the magazine 'Young Folks', 'Treasure Island' was to become one of the best-known and best-loved adventure stories in the world.

A boozy old buccaneer called Billy Bones comes to stay at the lonely inn, run by young Jim Hawkins and his mother. His fellow-pirates, led by the sinister Long John Silver come after him and tip him the dreaded 'black spot', the pirate death-threat. They're after

the map that leads to Captain Flint's treasure. When Bones is killed, young Jim finds the map. He sets sail, with the Doctor and the Squire in a ship called the 'Hispaniola'. Little do they know that half their crew are pirates – and that the one-legged ship's cook, with his crutch and the parrot on his shoulder, crying 'Pieces of eight! Pieces of eight!' is none other than Long John Silver himself!

Much filmed and televised, and turned into an ever-popular play, 'Treasure Island' has become a legend. Its sinister pirates' chorus still echoes in the world's imagination:

'Fifteen men on the dead man's chest
Yo-ho-ho and a bottle of rum!
Drink and the devil had done for the rest –
Yo-ho-ho and a bottle of rum!'

Jekyll and Hyde

In 1885, RLS settled in Bournemouth. Stevenson created another legend with 'The Strange Case of Dr Jekyll and Mr Hyde'. Kindly Dr Jekyll invents the potion that liberates the repressed evil that lurks in all of us. Under the influence of the potion he changes into horrible Mr Hyde, who rampages about Victorian London committing numerous dirty deeds. The expression 'a Jekyll and Hyde personality' has passed into the English language. In later years the book was

'I Know who you are – you're Jeremy Beadle!'

frequently filmed, with many a famous film star tackling the transformation from the good and handsome Jekyll to the hideous and evil Hyde. (In the Hammer Horror film version, 'Dr Jekyll and *Sister* Hyde', poor old Jekyll even suffered a sex change – I bet that cut him off short!)

'Kidnapped' and 'Catriona'

Stevenson wrote two more famous adventure stories, both set in the eighteenth century. 'Kidnapped' tells how young David Balfour foils the schemes of his evil uncle and claims his inheritance, helped by the 'bonny fighter' Alan Breck.

'The Master of Ballantrae' with its fascinating hero-villain was another Scottish historical adventure. As well as his novels, Stevenson wrote a number of short stories although he actually started it in 1887, when he went to the USA. Many, like 'Markheim' and the spooky 'Thrawn Janet' are still remembered today. He wrote poetry and published several collections of essays.

South Sea Adventure

In 1887 Stevenson set off on a real-life adventure to match anything in his books. He and his family went to the USA and from there chartered a schooner and sailed for the South Seas, looking for a climate that would suit Stevenson's still-failing health. They settled in Samoa, where Stevenson ended his days. He became a famous local figure, known to the natives as 'Tusitala' – The Teller of Tales.

With his stepson, Lloyd Osbourne, Stevenson wrote two more adventure stories, 'The Wrecker' and 'The Ebb Tide.' His last, and potentially greatest work, 'Weir of Hermiston', was a study of father-son conflict – perhaps a working out of his own early difficulties with his dad. Sadly, it was unfinished when he died, still in his early forties, in 1894.

A Life of Adventure

Stevenson pulled off a rare feat in the writing game, turning out tales of exciting adventure that were literary masterpieces too. He packed a lot into a relatively short time. Despite poor health, he enjoyed a life of travel and adventure, and he had a long and happy marriage. He wrote novels, essays and much fine poetry as well.

He even wrote his own epitaph:

'Under the wide and starry sky
Dig the grave and let me lie.
Glad did I live, and gladly die,
And I laid me down with a will.
This be the verse you grave for me
Here he lies where he longed to be
Home is the sailor, home from sea
And the hunter home from the hill . . .'

Chapter Twenty

OSCAR WILDE
1854–1900

Oscar the Great

Oscar Wilde – Oscar Fingal O'Flahertie Wills Wilde to give him his full name – is a fine example of the popular saying that all the best English writers are really Irish. (Well, it's popular in Ireland, anyway.) He was born in Dublin, the son of a successful surgeon, Sir William Wilde. His mum gave literary parties and wrote revolutionary poetry.

A high-flyer from the start, Oscar was educated at Trinity College, Dublin, and at Magdalen College, Oxford, where he won the Newdigate Prize for poetry and took a first-class degree.

Oscar Goes to Town

Oscar arrived in London with a ready-made reputation as a wit and poet. He dressed outrageously, talked flamboyantly, collected peacock's feathers and declared himself a believer in 'Art for Art's sake'.

A wild Irishman sneaked up behind me and pinched my feathers

That was Wilde.

He was what was known as an aesthete – the sort of young man who turns up today in arts programmes on the telly. In 1881 he published a volume of poetry, and by 1882 he was off on a lecture tour of America. Going through American Customs he was asked if he had anything to declare. 'I have nothing to declare except my genius,' said Oscar loftily.

Wilde enjoyed America. Writing about a Western town called Leadville, in his 'Impressions of America', he described a bar-room notice:

'Please do not shoot the pianist. He is doing his best.'

Oscar Settles Down

Soon after that, you may be surprised to learn, he married a lady called Constance Lloyd – they had two sons. He became the editor of a magazine, 'Woman's World'. He produced a book of fairy tales (no jokes please) called 'The Happy Prince'. He wrote a book of short stories 'Lord Arthur Savile's Crime' and his one and only novel, 'The Picture of Dorian Grey.' It's the story of a handsome but evil young man who *stays* young and handsome – despite years and years spent in every kind of wickedness and debauchery. Turns out he's got this picture of himself in his attic. Dorian doesn't change, but the picture

gets older and more evil every day. In the preface, Oscar spells out his artistic creed:

'There is no such thing as a moral or an immoral book. Books are well written or badly written.'

Oscar On Stage

Oscar's first attempts at drama, tragedies like 'Vera, or the Nihilists' and 'The Duchess of Padua' were all flops. Even the highly-coloured 'Salome' didn't do too well, though the famous Dance of the Seven Veils caused quite a scandal. Oscar tried another approach. Over the following years, he produced a string of brilliantly successful social comedies.

Lady Windermere and Others

In the first, 'Lady Windermere's Fan' there are such gems as:

'I can resist everything except temptation,'

and Oscar's famous definition of a cynic:

'A man who knows the price of everything, and the value of nothing.'

'A Woman of No Importance' has another famous definition, much quoted by today's anti-hunting lobby:

'The English country gentleman galloping after a fox – the unspeakable in full pursuit of the uneatable.'

The Importance of Being Earnest

The funniest, the most-successful and the most famous of all Oscar's plays, 'The Importance of Being Earnest' is still frequently read and performed today. Even the title is a joke. The heroine says she could never love a man unless his name was Ernest – which is tough on the hero, who thinks his name is Jack. (Luckily it turns out to be Ernest after all.) His girl-friend's mother, the formidable Lady Bracknell is far from pleased to learn that he's an orphan:

'To lose one parent, Mr Worthing, may be regarded as a misfortune; to lose both looks like carelessness.'

It doesn't help matters much when Jack explains that as a baby he was found in a handbag in a station cloakroom.

Lady Bracknell: *A handbag!*

(As delivered by Dame Edith Evans, and by a variety of other famous actresses, this two-word line is the biggest sure-fire laugh in the history of the theatre.)

Oscar's Downfall

So far Oscar's life sounds like one long success story. But, of course, he had a secret. He was gay or, strictly speaking, bisexual. Today it simply wouldn't matter much. Then, things were very different. Homosexuality was still a crime. It was possible to stay out of trouble by being discreet. But Oscar was colourful, flamboyant and openly camp. Worse still, he had a powerful enemy. One of Oscar's many fashionable friends was a young man called Lord Alfred Douglas, commonly known as Bosie. Bosie's father was the Marquess of Queensberry, a huntin', shootin' and fishin' peer of the old school, and bonkers into the bargain. Convinced that Oscar Wilde had seduced and corrupted his son, the Marquess set out to destroy him.

Oscar in Court

For a time Oscar ignored the Marquess's taunts, but when an insulting note was left at his club, Oscar sued the Marquess for libel. It was a fatal mistake. Oscar was up against the Establishment in full force, and his witty quips didn't go down too well in the dock. He lost the case. Shortly afterwards, Oscar was prosecuted 'for homo-sexual offences' and sentenced to two years' hard labour. He left a

'Prison food's so awful, it can make you feel queer!'

moving record of his suffering in his famous poem, 'The Ballad of Reading Gaol':

> *'I know not whether Laws be right*
> *Or whether Laws be wrong;*
> *All that we know who live in gaol*

Is that the walls are strong;
And that each day is like a year,
A year whose days are long.'

Wilde felt betrayed by his friends. The poem's tone is bitter:

'Yet each man kills the thing he loves,
By each let this be heard,
Some do it with a bitter look,
Some with a flattering word.
The coward does it with a kiss,
The brave man with a sword!'

On his release Wilde went to France, where he struggled with poverty and poor health for three more years (his wife stayed in England, didn't divorce him, but changed her name). Wilde was defiantly witty to the last: 'Paris has always been an expensive place to die,' he complained. 'Particularly for a foreigner . . .'

Presented with a big medical bill on his deathbed he said, 'I suppose that I shall have to die beyond my means . . .'

It is also said that his last words as he gazed at the hotel wallpaper were: 'Either it goes, or I go,' and he promptly died.

Oscar Wilde died in disgrace, in poverty and in exile. It was a sad end to a glittering career. But as long as somewhere on some stage an outraged Lady Bracknell exclaims, 'A handbag!' and the theatre explodes with laughter, poor old Oscar Wilde will never be entirely forgotten . . .

Chapter Twenty-one

GEORGE BERNARD SHAW
1856–1950

Another One for the Irish

George Bernard Shaw's career provides further evidence that all the best English writers are Irish. He was born in a Protestant family in Dublin, the son of a boozy dad and a musical mum. When Shaw was sixteen, his mother got fed up with waiting for dad to come home from the pub and made off to London with her two daughters. Shaw, who was working for a firm of land agents, stayed on in Ireland a few years longer. When he was twenty, he threw up his job and joined his mother and sisters in London, determined to become a writer.

He started by writing five novels, all flops. (Shaw himself reckoned he earned about nine quid in his first ten years as an author.) At the same time he was working hard to educate himself. He read Karl

'I've heard of GBH but what's GBS?'

Marx and became a life-long socialist. Naturally shy, he joined the Fabian Society, an early group of socialist intellectuals, and made himself into a brilliant public speaker. With his mother's help, he gradually built up a career as a music critic, writing under the unlikely name of Corno di Bassetto.

Shaw Takes the Stage

He became a theatre critic too, much influenced by the modern ideas of Norwegian playwright Henrik Ibsen. Shaw soon became disillusioned with the artificiality of the London stage, and decided he could do better. He was never exactly overburdened with modesty. In a later essay he wrote:

'With the single exception of Homer, there is no eminent writer, not even Sir Walter Scott, whom I can despise so entirely as I despise Shakespeare when I measure my mind against his.'

Shaw started writing a new kind of play – the play of ideas. Each of his plays deals with at least one big central theme.

Plays of Ideas

Shaw's first play, 'Widowers' Houses' is about the corruptions of capitalism. A Victorian gent is faced with the fact that the money which makes him rich and respectable comes from the rents on slum properties.

His next play, 'Mrs Warren's Profession' dealt with society's sexual hypocrisy, and the ethics of prostitution. This time he'd gone too far. Banned for the next ten years, the play wasn't actually staged until 1902. Undeterred Shaw went on writing in exactly the same style.

'Arms and the Man' deals with the reality as opposed to the myth of war. Its hero, Bluntschli is more concerned with scrounging food and staying alive than with death or glory.

'You can always tell an old soldier . . . The young ones carry pistols and cartridges, the old ones grub.'

Bluntschli himself keeps his ammunition pouches filled with chocolate. (The play was made into a successful musical – called 'The Chocolate Soldier'!)

THE CHOCOLATE SOLDIER

Shaw's Fair Lady

A later play, 'Pygmalion' dealt with the English class system, and the way we judge people by the way they talk. Perhaps the most popular of Shaw's plays, it tells how the arrogant Professor Higgins makes a bet that he can teach flower girl Eliza Doolittle to talk like a lady:

> *'Remember that you are a human being with a soul and the divine gift of articulate speech . . .'* he tells the baffled Eliza. *'Don't sit there crooning like a bilious pigeon!'*

Like many of Shaw's plays, 'Pygmalion' was successfully filmed. Later it was made into a hit musical, 'My Fair Lady'.

Shaw the Feminist

Many of Shaw's plays feature strong independent women – a pretty daring idea in those days. (When he started writing, women didn't even have the vote.) 'Caesar and Cleopatra' shows the young and impulsive Cleopatra being turned into a real queen by the older and wiser Julius Caesar, who teaches her to rule:

> *'Without punishment. Without revenge. Without judgement.'*

Other plays like 'Candida', 'Saint Joan' and his Salvation Army play, 'Major Barbara' all feature strong, independent-minded heroines. Shaw believed in something he called the Life Force, the blind power of evolution working through man. He saw women as the real carriers of this mysterious force. In most of his plays, they are stronger and more determined than the men. In 'Man and Superman' the revolutionary and would-be free spirit Tanner says:

'It is a woman's business to get married as soon as possible, and a man's to keep unmarried as long as he can.'

But the determined heroine, Ann, gets him in the end. She's got the Life Force on her side.

A Load of (Brilliant) Old Chat

Shaw covered every subject under the sun in his plays, from Irish politics in 'John Bull's Other Island' to medical ethics in 'The Doctor's Dilemma'. He was fascinated by ideas of every kind, political, philosophical, and even religious. Not a lot actually happens in his plays. Mostly people just stand around and argue. This could have made for a lot of amazingly boring message plays – but Shaw is anything but boring. Luckily for him, and for us, he was a born dramatist with a strong comic sense. He creates wonderful characters and writes hilariously comic scenes. His bad characters get even better lines than his good ones. In 'Pygmalion' Eliza's disreputable father says:

'I'm one of the undeserving *poor, that's what I am. Think what that means to a man . . . he's up agen middle class mortality all the time.'*

Public Shaw

Over the years, Shaw slowly turned into a celebrity. He was active in politics and he wrote and lectured endlessly. The tall thin bearded figure popped up everywhere. He visited the front in the First World War, won the Nobel Prize for Literature in 1925, visited Stalin's Russia in 1931, and survived to see World War Two, the defeat of Hitler, the post-war Labour Government, and the start of the NHS.

Shaw in Private

There's not much to say about Shaw's private life – largely because he didn't really have one. He lived his life on stage, in the public eye, and he was only really interested in ideas. A lifelong vegetarian and teetotaller, he didn't seem to have any vices at all. (Nudge, nudge, wink, wink, know what I mean?) There were lots of adoring lady disciples, and flirtations with society hostesses and famous actresses – but Shaw kept everything firmly on the mental plane.

When he was ill in 1898 an Irish heiress called Charlotte moved in to look after him. Shaw married her to avoid a scandal and they lived happily but platonically together for the next forty-five years.

The Grandest Old Man

George Bernard Shaw lived to the amazing age of ninety-four – there must be something in this vegetarian lark after all. He kept on writing almost to the end, publishing 'Everybody's Political What's What' when he was over ninety. Busy and active to the last, he was pruning trees in his garden when he had a fall. He died on November 2nd 1950, one of the grandest, and certainly the oldest, of Eng Lit's Grand Old Men.

Chapter Twenty-two

SIR ARTHUR CONAN DOYLE
1859–1930

Young Doctor Doyle

In 1881 a new doctor arrived in the sleepy little seaside town of Southsea. He was a jolly giant of a man, keen on cricket and boxing. Business was slow – maybe the seaside air kept everyone healthy. Doyle, who'd already sold a few short stories to magazines, tried to make a bit extra by writing. In 1886 he tried his hand at a detective story, called 'A Study in Scarlet'.

The Great Detective

Doyle invented an eccentric detective, a thin, hawk-faced man with a brilliant mind and a number of weird habits. He plays the violin when he's thinking, smokes like a chimney, and works like a demon when he's on an interesting case. When he's bored he sometimes turns to: *'a seven per cent solution of cocaine'*. (It might seem

strange of Doyle to make his detective hero a part-time junkie, but the Victorians had an amazingly casual attitude to drugs. The founder of psychoanalysis, Sigmund Freud, used to dose depressed patients with cocaine – he discovered it cheered them up no end . . .)

A Study in Scarlet

The narrator of 'A Study in Scarlet' is a certain Dr Watson. Like his creator, he's decent, straightforward, and utterly British. Formerly an army doctor, Watson has been wounded in Afghanistan and sent home to live on a tiny pension. To cut down on expenses, he arranges to share a set of rooms in Baker Street. His flatmate, an eccentric character called Sherlock Holmes, is the world's first Consulting Detective. Sherlock Holmes is a man with amazing

powers. Called in on a mysterious murder, he studies the scene of the crime and dazzles the cops:

> *'The murderer . . . was more than six feet high, was in the prime of life, had small feet for his height, wore coarse square-toed boots and smoked a Trichinopoly cigar. He came here with his victim in a four-wheeled cab . . . In all probability the murderer had a florid face and the finger-nails of his right hand were remarkably long. These are only a few indications, but they may assist you . . .'*

Dinner with Oscar

Doyle sold 'A Study in Scarlet' for a measly twenty-five quid. The publishers said they couldn't put it out right away – 'the market is currently flooded with cheap fiction'. Then an American publisher called Lippincott, in London looking for promising writers, took Doyle and another young chap called Oscar Wilde out to dinner. (I wonder how they got on?)

The meal, surely the most successful nosh-up in publishing history, produced Wilde's 'Picture of Dorian Grey' and Doyle's second Sherlock Holmes novel, 'The Sign of Four'.

'Arthur loves boxing and Oscar knows all about the Queensberry Rules – we should get along fine!'

From Disaster to Triumph

The second Holmes novel, like the first, did only moderately well. No-one was very interested in Doyle's eccentric detective – not even Doyle himself, who returned to his real love, the historical novel, with 'The White Company'. By now he had a wife and child to support – not to mention a mother, an invalid father, and seven brothers and sisters back home in Edinburgh. Hoping to boost his earnings, he moved to London and set up as an eye specialist. It was a disaster – he didn't get a single patient. Luckily the new 'Strand Magazine' was looking for fiction. Doyle decided to give his detective one last chance and wrote six Sherlock Holmes short stories. They were published from July to December 1891 – and the magazine's circulation shot up like a rocket. Sherlock Holmes was a hit!

Money from Holmes

Doyle demanded more money, bumping up his fee from thirty-six to fifty pounds per story. Writing at top speed, he produced a dozen more Sherlock Holmes stories. Published monthly throughout 1892, they were even more popular than the first batch.

But Doyle was already beginning to rebel against his over-successful creation. 'I think of slaying Holmes,' he wrote to his mother. 'He takes my mind from better things.' The 'Strand Magazine' waved lots more money at him, and Doyle dashed off another dozen tales. But in the last story of the series, 'The Final Problem' there was a shock in store for Sherlock's many admirers.

Locked in a final death-grapple with his arch-enemy Professor Moriarty, 'The Napoleon of International Crime', Holmes tumbled over the edge of the dreaded Reichenbach Falls. Readers set up howls of protest, but Doyle insisted that Holmes was dead and done with.

Despite his recent success, it was a trying time in Conan Doyle's life. His wife Louise caught tuberculosis. Doyle looked after her devotedly throughout her long illness. While she was ill Doyle fell deeply in love with a young woman called Jean Leckie, and she with him. As upright a Victorian gentleman as his own Dr Watson, Doyle kept their relationship strictly platonic. A year after Louise's death, Jean Leckie and Conan Doyle were married.

Sherlock's Comeback

Doyle was a public figure by now. He wrote innumerable non-Holmes short stories, historical novels and early science fiction classics, like 'The Lost World'. He served as a volunteer surgeon in the Boer War and was awarded a knighthood for his services. But wherever he went, people asked him about Sherlock Holmes. Holmes had been gone for over eight years by now, and Doyle was beginning to relent. In 1901 he published a Sherlock Holmes novel, 'The Hound of the Baskervilles'. Based on an old Dartmoor legend, the story tells of an old Devon family, cursed, because of an ancient crime, by a hound from hell. Now Sir Henry Baskerville is mysteriously dead. Footprints have been found beside the body. What kind of footprints?

'Mr Holmes, they were the footprints of a gigantic hound!'

Back from the Dead

Doyle insisted that Holmes was still dead – this was an earlier untold adventure. But then an American publisher, made him an offer he couldn't refuse – five thousand dollars *a story* to bring Sherlock Holmes back to life.

In October 1903, 'The Empty House' was published in the 'Strand Magazine' – and excited crowds mobbed the bookstalls. Holmes it seems, hadn't gone over the falls after all. It was all a plot to fool Moriarty's gang. The dauntless duo were back on the trail. Conan Doyle had finally come to terms with his immortal creation. Several more story collections followed, until Holmes finally retired to the Sussex Downs to keep bees. Even then Doyle brought him out of retirement one last time. In 1914, at the beginning of World War One, Holmes nobbled Von Bork, the German master spy.

Sherlock Lives

Sherlock Holmes, of course, is still going strong. There have been several Sherlock Holmes stage plays, innumerable films, radio and television dramatisations. What is the amazing appeal of Sherlock Holmes? The plots of some of the stories are pretty thin, and Sherlock's deductions verge on the miraculous. Raymond Chandler, the famous American hard-boiled thriller writer said it was 'An atmosphere, and a few lines of unforgettable dialogue.' In the story 'Silver Blaze' Holmes draws the attention of the baffled Inspector (Inspectors are *always* baffled in Sherlock Holmes stories), to:

'The curious incident of the dog in the night time.'
'The dog did nothing in the night time.'
'That was the curious incident,' remarked Sherlock Holmes.'

(The dog didn't bark because it *knew* the intruder, geddit?)

In 'The Norwood Builder' Holmes takes a quick glance at a new client and says coolly,

'You mentioned your name as if I should recognise it, but beyond the obvious facts that you are a bachelor, a solicitor, a Freemason and an asthmatic, I know nothing whatever about you.'

(In other stories we see Holmes deduce the owners complete life-history from a hat, a walking-stick or a watch.)

But perhaps it's the atmosphere after all that matters most. Christopher Morley, distinguished American critic and Sherlock

116

Holmes fan, sums it up best: 'Let it be a stormy winter morning, when Holmes routs Watson out of bed in haste. The Doctor wakes to see that tall ascetic figure by the bedside with a candle. "Come, Watson, come! The game is afoot!"'

' Come, Watson, come! The game is afoot!'

Into the Unknown

In 1916 Doyle attended a seance and became convinced that he had communicated with the spirit of his wife's dead brother. He became a passionate propagandist for the spiritualist cause, lecturing world-wide and writing innumerable books and pamphlets. Doyle died in 1930, over seventy years old.

Chapter Twenty-three

RUDYARD KIPLING
1865–1936

East of Suez

Kipling's name will always be associated with India and the East –
even though he spent most of his life in England or America. He was
born in Bombay, the son of artist and sculptor John Lockwood
Kipling, who taught in the new Art School. Young Ruddy had an
idyllically happy childhood. His early years were soaked in the exotic
sights and sounds of Bombay. When he was little he spoke and
thought in Hindi. No wonder – he saw more of his *ayah*, his Indian
nurse, than he did of his parents.

'I'm so pleased young Ruddy is absorbing some Indian Culture John'

Home to Hell

When Kipling was six, his mother took him back to England. She
deposited him and his younger sister, Trixie, with foster parents in
Southsea, and then rejoined her husband in India. This was
common practice at the time – but unfortunately for Kipling, his
foster mother took against him. He was bullied, humiliated, called a

habitual liar, and often beaten. It took his mother six years to realise what was going on. In 1877 she came back to England and took him away. (Kipling described this unhappy period of his life in a harrowing short story, 'Baa, Baa, Black Sheep.')

Westward Ho!

After Southsea, Kipling was packed off to boarding school at Westward Ho! in Devon. The United Services College was a cut-price public school, founded for the children of army officers. There was frequent use of the cane, and quite a bit of bullying. But although Kipling was smallish and short-sighted, he was stocky and tough as well. He survived to become the 'school writer', running and writing most of the school magazine. He shared a study with two other boys and their adventures are told in Kipling's famous school story, 'Stalky and Co'. Stalky is the cunning, tough-minded leader, M'Turk the sharp-tongued Irish intellectual, and Beetle is the bespectacled would-be poet, whom Kipling bases on himself.

Back to India

In 1882 Kipling returned to India, as a trainee journalist on the 'Civil and Military Gazette' in Lahore. He toiled in India for the next seven years, enduring long hours, boredom, and unbearable heat. He began to write, recording the lives of the British soldiers, civil servants and civilians who ruled in India. He published a little book of poems, 'Departmental Ditties' and some short stories, 'Plain Tales from the Hills'. Kipling's fame spread rapidly across India. In 1889, still only 24, he decided to go home to England and build a career as a writer.

Home Again

Kipling arrived in London with the backing of a fast-growing reputation. His stories were beginning to be published in English magazines. So too were his amazingly-popular 'Barrack Room Ballads', poems in Cockney dialect about Army life. Perhaps the most famous is the wounded soldier's tribute to the humble water-carrier who sacrifices his life to bring him a drink:

'Though I've belted you an' flayed you
By the living Gawd that made you
You're a better man than I am, Gunga Din!'

119

More of his Indian short stories appeared in collections like 'Soldier's Three'. He even wrote a couple of novels, 'The Light that Failed', about a blinded war-artist who seeks death in battle, and 'The Naulakha', about a fabulously valuable necklace.

Kipling and Carrie

This second novel was written in collaboration with a young American publisher called Wolcott Balestier, with whom Kipling had become close friends. Wolcott had a sister, a small determined young woman called Carrie. A year after publication, Wolcott died suddenly of typhoid. Soon afterwards, Kipling married Carrie – or perhaps she married him. She certainly ran his life from then on, doing his accounts, fixing his appointments, protecting him from visitors. Incidentally, Kipling has been accused of less than favourable attitudes to women. He describes a glamorous vamp as:

'A rag, a bone, and a hank of hair'.

There's:

'The female of the species is more deadly than the male.'

And:

'A woman is only a woman, but a good cigar is a smoke.'

Off to America

Kipling and Carrie went to visit Carrie's family in Vermont and Kipling, or maybe Carrie, decided to stay. They built a house and lived there for the next four years. During this time Kipling wrote

'Mowgli's very backward – when I was his age, I was chasing bitches!'

his famous 'The Jungle Book' and its sequel called, believe it or not, 'The Second Jungle Book'. Most of the stories concern the adventures of Mowgli, who gets lost in the jungle as a baby and is adopted by a pack of wolves. With Baloo the bear and Bagheera the black panther as his teacher, he grows up to become a kind of king of the jungle, and to kill his deadly enemy, the man-eating tiger Shere Khan, before returning to live with men.

Residence in Vermont ended unhappily in 1896, after Kipling had a public row with Carrie's drunken brother Beattie which ended up in court. When the case was over, the Kiplings headed for home.

England Again

Back home in England, Kipling settled down to find his roots, eventually buying a house called 'Batemans' in Sussex. By now his fame was increasing steadily, and the shy publicity-hating Kipling was becoming a celebrity. He was a great friend of H Rider Haggard, who wrote 'King Solomon's Mines'. A poet of the day, irritated by the famous pair, looked forward to a time:

'When the Rudyards cease from Kipling
And the Haggards ride no more!'

In 1897 he wrote 'Captains Courageous'. A spoiled rich boy falls overboard on a cruise. He's rescued by a fishing-smack, and has to work his passage home – naturally, it makes a man of him. In 1899, 'Stalky and Co' appeared. The 'Grange Hill' of its day, it was severely criticised for the 'horrible vileness' of its picture of English public school life. More popular were the 'Just So Stories', fantastic animal fables for little kids – like 'How the Elephant Got His Trunk' (the crocodile pulled his nose!).

'Dop pulling my dose!'

In 1901, Kipling produced his one truly great novel. 'Kim' is the story of an orphaned English boy who grows up as a tough, cunning, streetwise kid amongst Indians. His parentage is discovered and he is educated as an Englishman, much against his will. Later he returns to travel the roads and hills of his beloved India, as a secret service agent. With its wonderfully colourful account of Indian life, and its examination of what it means to be Indian and to be English, Kim is an undoubted masterpiece. The distinguished Indian critic Chaudhuri said it was the finest book about India ever written.

Triumph and Disaster

Kipling continued to grow in stature as a public figure, though fame couldn't protect him from family tragedy. In 1899 on a visit to New York, Kipling and his little daughter fell ill with pneumonia. Kipling recovered but his daughter died. Her loss haunted him for the rest of his life. In 1906 he published 'Puck of Pook's Hill' in which two children, Dan and Una, meet the fairy Puck, who conjures up figures from the past to tell them of England's history. A sequel, 'Rewards and Fairies' appeared four years later. In 1907 Kipling was the first English writer to be awarded the Nobel Prize for Literature. He was several times asked to be Poet Laureate, but always refused, feeling he should preserve his independence. Tragedy struck again in the First World War. His son John was killed in action in 1915. Kipling wrote a moving poem:

> *'These were our children who died for our lands . . .*
> *But who shall return us the children . . .'*

Kipling Carries On

Kipling went on working steadily, producing story collections like 'Traffics and Discoveries', 'Debits and Credits', and 'Limits and Renewals'. His last work was an autobiography, 'Something of Myself'. Kipling was so protective of his privacy that it should have been called, 'Hardly Anything of Myself'. Towards the end of the book, Kipling slips quietly into the past tense. It's a real shock when the last sentence of the book refers to the kind of atlas globe:

> *'. . . which was still in use for some years after my death.'*

Kipling died three weeks later on January 18th, 1936. There was world-wide mourning, and his ashes were laid in Poets Corner in Westminster Abbey.

You can still buy framed copies of his most famous poem 'If' which gives you all the rules for a completely successful life; it starts:

> *'If you can keep your head when all about you*
> *Are losing theirs, and blaming it on you . . .'*

and ends:

> '*If you can fill the unforgiving minute*
> *With sixty seconds' worth of distance run,*
> *Yours is the Earth, and everything that's in it,*
> *And – which is more – you'll be a man, my son!*'

(There you are – simple, really . . .)

Chapter Twenty-four

H G WELLS
1866–1946

Wells and Tomorrow's World

Herbert George Wells represents a new kind of writer. Ruthless bloodsucking capitalists though they were (sorry, Maggie), the Victorians were genuinely keen on encouraging enterprise. For the first time, educational opportunities were becoming available for everyone. If you were exceptionally bright and worked incredibly hard, it was possible to climb the social ladder. From humble beginnings, H G fought his way up to fame and fortune.

Educating Herbert

Wells's father was an unsuccessful shopkeeper and part-time professional cricketer. His mother was a ladies' maid, who later became housekeeper in a big country house called Up Park. Young Herbert left school at fourteen and became an apprentice in a draper's shop, selling 'soft goods' – curtain materials, furnishing fabrics and so on.

SOFT FURNISHINGS

'If I stay here it'll be curtains for me!'

Wells hated the drapery trade. Unqualified as he was, he wangled a job as a pupil-teacher in a nearby school. He studied hard in his spare time and got a scholarship to the Normal School of Science in

Kensington. By now he was just as interested in literature as in science. He spent time reading literary classics when he should have been studying scientific textbooks. He made lots of new friends, hard-up young students like himself, and became interested in socialism. Literature and politics combined to sabotage Wells's studies. At the end of his third year, he failed his degree.

Fighting Back

To make matters worse, he was struck down by lung trouble. When he recovered, Wells was forced to take teaching jobs so he could write in his spare time. He went to lodge with his aunt, and fell in love with his pretty young cousin Isabel – who refused to marry him till he had a respectable job. After teaching in some pretty ghastly schools, Wells finished up working for the Universal Tutorial College, a sort of combined crammer and correspondence college. In his spare time he studied for his external degree at London University. It was a long hard struggle but he made it, passing with first-class honours. He was promoted at his Tutorial College, and in 1891 he married Isabel.

Starting Again

For anyone else this might have been a happy ending, but not for Wells. He was determined to be somebody – and he didn't mean just a tutor at a tutorial college. His marriage went wrong almost from the start. He'd fallen for Isabel because she was a pretty girl living in the same house. (As the Americans say, nothing propinks like propinquity.) Once married, they found they'd almost nothing in common. Isabel was a quiet conventional girl, who wanted a quiet

Apart from science and literature I could help you with your sex education Miss Robbins!'

conventional life. Wells was excitable, passionate and ambitious. He reacted to his unsatisfactory marriage by starting a relationship with one of his students, an attractive intellectual girl called Amy Robbins.

Wells tackled the career problem by writing essays, short stories and articles on popular science for publications like the 'Pall Mall

Gazette'. As his career prospered, things at home got worse – and so did H G's health. He began to fear he was destined to die young, without ever knowing true greatness or real happiness. In 1894 Wells left his wife and eloped with Amy. A year later, when his divorce was finalised, they were married.

Scientific Romances

Wells's background in science meant he could write a new kind of story – the Scientific Romance. He began with 'The Time Machine', which is both science fiction and social allegory. In the far distant future, humanity has evolved into two different species, the decadent Eloi, and the brutish Morlocks upon whom they feed – literally. (The nobs exploiting the workers, geddit?) 'The Time Machine' was a great success – and so were such later books as 'The Island of Doctor Moreau' in which genetic experimentation produces beastmen, and 'The Invisible Man', which inspired numerous films and television series and a classic music-hall routine:

'The Invisible Man's outside.'

'Well, tell him I can't see him!'

'Normally I'm invisible officer but I've unexpectedly materialized today!'

Wells's most famous piece of sci-fi, 'The War of the Worlds', was published in 1898. Alien intellects, 'vast, cool and unsympathetic', were watching us from outer space. The many-tentacled Martians invade, in their three-legged fighting machines, and wipe out Earth's armies with their death-ray (all right, I know it's corny, but it was all new stuff at the time). Then the invaders collapse – clobbered by Earth's germs. Forty years later, 'The War of the Worlds' was to freak out America, dramatised and updated on radio by the young

Orson Welles. People thought it was really happening, and fled in their thousands.

Real Life Scandal

After the success of his 'Scientific Romances' Wells turned to stories of real life, usually based pretty closely on his own. 'Love and Mr Lewisham' is the tale of a struggling young teacher who feels trapped by marriage. The humble life of 'Kipps', a little draper's shop-assistant with a poetic soul is transformed, and almost ruined, by sudden prosperity. 'Ann Veronica' is a strong-minded young woman who defies society by running off with the man she loves, even though he's married. This last book nearly ruined Wells's reputation. 'The Spectator' said it was 'capable of poisoning the minds of those who read it', and accused Wells of depicting, 'animal yearning or lust' in 'a community of scuffling stoats and ferrets.'

Popular Mr Polly

For a time Wells was clobbered by the Establishment. Not that it worried him very much – he rather enjoyed it. He regained his popularity with 'The History of Mr Polly' in which another of his frustrated little men a small shopkeeper, not unlike Wells's own father, rebels, sets fire to his shop, and goes off to find freedom at the riverside 'Potwell Inn'.

Wells and World Affairs

All this time, Wells kept up his interest in socialism. He joined the Fabian Society, and was soon locked in furious arguments with his fellow members – especially a tall, skinny red-bearded Irishman called George Bernard Shaw. Much of Wells's writing was political too, a stream of essays and articles, and books like his massive, and massively popular, 'Outline of History'. He also kept up his interest in the opposite sex. Although his second marriage was far happier than his first, Wells still wandered from time to time – well, for most of the time, actually. (When young, Wells was a spindly little chap with glasses and a wispy moustache. As he grew older, he turned into a tubby little chap with glasses and a scrubby moustache. Yet throughout his life, beautiful and intelligent women found him irresistible. It must have been his giant brain – maybe size does matter after all!)

His most famous affair was with the writer Rebecca West. She wrote him a letter attacking his views, Wells asked her down for the weekend, and they soon resolved their differences in more ways than one. Despite all this constant carrying-on, Wells was genuinely devoted to his wife. They stayed happily married for over thirty years and he was desolated by her death.

'I'm a very sick man Rebecca except for my healthy interest in sex!'

Grand Old Wells

Although plagued for much of his life by poor health, Wells lived to be yet another Grand Old Man, always slightly upstaged by his friendly enemy Shaw. In 1936, when Wells was seventy, PEN, the famous literary society gave a dinner in his honour. And who proposed the toast? George Bernard Shaw, still full of beans at eighty, cheekily calling the guest of honour 'poor old Wells!' H G Wells lived till 1946. Long enough to see the establishment, in England at least, of the socialist state that had always been his dream. Long enough too to see the dropping of the atomic bomb at Hiroshima. It was a bitter moment for Wells. The science he had always loved had given mankind the power to destroy itself. One of Wells's friends was the famous Catholic writer G K Chesterton. Wells, a life-long unbeliever, once said in a letter that if Chesterton was right after all about God and the after-life, 'I shall always be able to pass into Heaven (if I want to) as a friend of GKC's.' Chesterton generously wrote back saying that if Wells ever did get to Heaven it would be 'Not by being a friend of mine, but a friend of Man.' It's not a bad description of the generous, determined, hard-working and idealistic H G Wells.

A friend of Man – not forgetting Woman of course . . .

Chapter Twenty-five

JAMES JOYCE
1882–1941

Another One for the Irish!

Like Wilde and Shaw, James Joyce fits into that 'all the best English writers are Irish' theory. He was born in Dublin, into a big family with the traditional hard-working mum and charming, drunken dad. Joyce was a bright, rebellious boy from the very first and his father made sure he got a good education. In 1898 Joyce entered University College, Dublin, where he soon got into trouble for rejecting religious studies for the works of new European dramatists like Ibsen. In 1902 James Joyce left Dublin for Paris to study medicine. He enjoyed life in Paris but he had to return to Dublin when his mother became badly ill. After her death, Joyce divided his time between boozing with fellow medical students and struggling to get started as a writer.

Dublin Days

In Joyce's autobiographical novel 'Portrait of the Artist as a Young Man', Stephen Dedalus, like his creator, is sensitive, spindly, and short-sighted. He struggles with religious doubts, and sexual urges,

'Write it all down my son — it could be a best seller!'

discovers art and literature, and has an almost mystical first-experience of sex with a young Dublin prostitute. Filled with guilt he repents and thinks of entering the priesthood. Finally he comes to realise that he can only find fulfilment as an artist, and decides to leave Dublin and go abroad to *'forge his soul.'* 'Portrait of the Artist' is a young man's book, redeemed by the clarity and vividness of the writing.

Abroad with Norah Barnacle

The time Joyce spent boozing in the Dublin pubs was to provide him with his greatest inspiration. On June 16th 1904 he met a barmaid with the splendid name of Norah Barnacle. They fell in love and the

'Ah you're pure genius Norah!'

following October they ran off together to Zurich. They stayed together for the rest of Joyce's life and married, a little belatedly in 1931 – they had two children by then. Throughout this time they lived on the Continent, first in Zurich and later in Trieste. Joyce carried on with his writing, supporting himself by working as an English teacher.

As well as 'Portrait of the Artist' Joyce produced a volume of poetry, and a book of short stories called 'Dubliners', about the frustrations of Irish life. But his real claims to fame are two massive experimental novels, 'Ulysses' and 'Finnegans Wake'.

Amazing Ulysses

The leading characters in 'Ulysses' are Leopold Bloom, a timid Jewish advertisement salesman, his voluptuous wife Molly – a character based firmly on Norah Barnacle – and Stephen Dedalus from 'Portrait of the Artist'. The novel's events all take place on one day in Dublin. The story moves through a public bath, a newspaper office, a library, several pubs, a maternity hospital, and a brothel, and introduces an amazing variety of Dublin themes and characters.

It uses a variety of styles and techniques from the good old 'stream of consciousness' through parody, realism, and fantasy. The one day in Dublin stands for all human life and Bloom, the archetypal 'little man', represents all mankind. Stephen, who he meets only at the end of the book, is the son he always wanted. The pattern of the book is loosely based on the 'Odyssey' by the classical Greek writer Homer.

Sexy Molly

'Ulysses' is an amazing work, rich, colourful, complicated and hilariously funny. Its publication caused an amazing amount of fuss. It was the naughty bits that caused all the trouble, particularly Molly Bloom's long sexy soliloquy at the end as she recalls the first time she made love:

> *'And I thought well as well him as another and then I asked him with my eyes to ask again yes and then he asked me would I yes to say yes my mountain flower and first I put my arms around him yes and drew him down to me so he could feel my breasts all perfume yes and his heart was going like mad and yes I said yes I will Yes.'*

'Read me Molly's sexy soliloquy...'   'No, No, no, no...!'

The book was published in Paris in 1922 without any trouble. (What would you expect from all those sex-mad frogs?) But the pure-minded New York post office authorities were so shocked that they burned the copies of the first English language edition. Not to be outdone, Folkstone customs officials seized the second edition in 1923. For the next thirteen years English readers had to make do with copies smuggled in from the sinful Continent. 'Ulysses' was finally published in England in 1936, and in America a year later.

Fantastic Finnegan

James Joyce's second epic is the even more fantastic 'Finnegans Wake', published in 1939. For this book Joyce created a language of

131

his own, using puns, obscure allusions and made-up words. The book's opening words are:

'*riverun, past Eve and Adam's, from swerve of shore to bend of bay brings us by a commodious vicus of recirculation, back to Howth Castle and Environs.*'

Later on come such coinages as:

'*All moanday, tearsday, wailsday, thumpsday, frightday, shatterday.*'

Someone is described as having

'*a base barreltone voice.*'

While 'Ulysses' took place all in one day, 'Finnegans Wake' takes place all in one night – and all in the mind of a Dublin pub owner called Humphrey Chimpden Earwicker – HCE for short. The initials also stand for Here Comes Everybody. The novel's themes are the recurring cycles of man's universal history, and the inner life of the artist. 'Finnegans Wake' is an amazing eccentric achievement. You could call it the ultimate Irish joke. It was published to a baffled and angry reception, but today it's recognised as a uniquely original work of genius.

Hard Times for Joyce

An exile all his life, Joyce moved from place to place on the Continent, usually hard up. Much of his work was published in instalments in magazines and his reputation grew only very slowly. Joyce made very little money from his writing. From time to time better-off friends and patrons helped him out. James Joyce suffered constantly from poor eyesight and had to have a long series of eye operations. In addition he was constantly worried about the mental health of his daughter. She had a severe nervous breakdown in 1932, and was later diagnosed as an incurable schizophrenic. Eventually Joyce's own health gave way. He had surgery for a duodenal ulcer, and never really recovered. He died in 1941, and was buried in Zurich.

Portrait of the Artist

Now over fifty years after his death, the stubborn, short-sighted little Irishman is recognised as one of the world's greatest writers. 'Ulysses' in particular is an acknowledged masterpiece. Throughout all his struggles and hard times, James Joyce never gave up. He achieved what his character Stephen Dedalus set out to do, breaking free of the petty restrictions of nineteenth-century Dublin life, and forging his soul as an artist.

Chapter Twenty-six

VIRGINIA WOOLF
1882–1941

A Literary Lady

It's scarcely surprising that Virginia Woolf led a literary life. She was born into a literary family, and grew up surrounded by artistic types. The poor girl never stood a chance – she was doomed to be a writer!

Her father was Sir Leslie Stephen, a literary journalist, philosopher and critic. He was the editor of the 'Dictionary of National Biography' and one of the cultural big shots of his day. Virginia was educated at home by her parents. When she was thirteen, her mother died and Virginia experienced the first of the bouts of depression that were to trouble her all her life. Grief-stricken by the loss of his wife, Sir Leslie died nine years later in 1904. After his death the now grown-up Stephen children moved to a house in London's Bloomsbury.

Bloomsbury Circus

The house eventually became the centre of a group of young intellectuals called 'The Bloomsbury Group' – the bright and brainy young things of their time. The group grew to include such names as the economist John Maynard Keynes, Lytton Strachey the historian, and writers like T S Eliot, E M Forster, Katherine Mansfield, Harold Nicolson, Vita Sackville-West and the Sitwells. The Bloomsbury Group's artistic achievements, their frequent feuds and rivalries and their never-ending series of affairs, form a high-powered literary soap-opera, endlessly studied and written about by later critics. There were constant romances, marriages, divorces, seductions and they were always running off with each other's wives or husbands regardless of sex. (You might say a gay old time was often had by all.)

Virginia's Career

Virginia herself was soon reviewing for the 'Times Literary Supplement' and, naturally, starting work on her first novel. In 1907 she married the writer Leonard Woolf and together they founded the Hogarth Press. He recognised her talent, and helped and supported her through many difficult years. Virginia Woolf's early novels, like 'The Voyage Out' and 'Night and Day' were okay but ordinary. It's for her later, more experimental work that she's now remembered.

A New Kind of Novel

In 1922 she published 'Jacob's Room' using a poetic, impressionistic style that was quite different from the conventional novel. Her poetical mate T S Eliot thought it was wonderful, but critics of the time attacked its lack of plot. 'Jacob's Room' was followed in 1925 by 'Mrs Dalloway'. The action, if that's the word, of the novel, takes place in one day, most of it inside the head of Clarissa Dalloway, the wife of an MP. We follow her thoughts as she goes off to buy flowers

'Sorry – we don't know any Greek songs, but we can do a little bit of Greek dancing!'

for the party which forms the climax of the book. She thinks about her husband, about a rival political hostess, about society acquaintances, an old suitor returned from abroad, a childhood friend . . . Clarissa's thoughts are contrasted with those of crazy shell-shocked Septimus, who thinks the sparrows in the park are singing in Greek. Septimus eventually jumps out of the window – the main, and almost the only bit of action in the book. The news is brought to Clarissa's party by his doctor . . .

The Lighthouse . . .

In 'To the Lighthouse' Mr and Mrs Ramsay, their family and friends are on holiday by the sea. They plan an expedition to the nearby lighthouse on the next day. Mr Ramsay decides the weather will be

'You'd thought, as a member of "the Bloomsbury Group", Virginia would write something more titillating than a trip to a Lighthouse.'

too rough, the trip is cancelled and the kids are fed up. The holiday ends, time passes, and the empty holiday house and gardens decay. Ten years later, Mr Ramsay, his children and some friends return. Mrs Ramsay has died in the meantime and Mr Ramsay is devastated by her death. This time the weather is fine, and the long-postponed trip to the lighthouse takes place at last . . . That's it really. Two days by the sea and a cancelled boat-trip that takes place ten years later. Not exactly a ripping yarn – but moods, emotions and the contradictions of character are precisely portrayed.

Mr Ramsay, for example, is a distinguished philosopher and a genuinely great man. But he's arrogant and unfeeling with his children, and depends on his wife for emotional support. Mrs Ramsay is a good, kind-hearted woman with a gift for making people happy. Yet she's far too fond of interfering in other people's lives. The differing characters of the Ramsay children, the guests and holiday acquaintances all emerge with enormous clarity.

The third of Virginia Woolf's more experimental novels is 'The Waves'. It traces the lives of a group of friends, largely through their own thoughts and reflections. The novel is divided by a number of poetic passages describing sunrise and sunset over the sea. Even more than most of her books it's not so much a novel as a kind of prose poem.

Ups and Downs

Although at her best she could be cheerful and sociable, a period of depression usually followed the end of each novel. Sometimes she

tried to cheer herself up by tackling lighter works, such as 'Flush' a biography of Elizabeth Barrett Browning's pet spaniel. She was actively interested in feminism all her life. Her essay 'A Room of One's Own' is not only a statement of the feminist position but a plea for common ground between the sexes:

'Perhaps a mind that is purely masculine cannot create, any more than a mind that is purely feminine . . .'

A Sad End

Despite recurring bouts of mental illness, Virginia Woolf managed to produce nine novels, and a number of short stories, articles and essays. Sadly, it all got too much for her in the end. In 1941 she'd just finished writing 'Between the Acts', and the resulting depression was even worse than usual. It was a black time. The war, the second in her lifetime, was going badly and her home in London had just been flattened in the bombing. One day she went out for a walk, filled her pockets with stones, and threw herself into the river.

Who's Afraid of Virginia Woolf?

Ironically, her name is often remembered today because of Edward Albee's savagely satirical play about the stormy marriage of an American professor and his wife. Virginia Woolf's books can be complex and difficult and she herself sometimes wondered if they could really be called novels at all. She wasn't much bothered about the traditional business of story telling. Instead she concentrated on capturing mood, character, atmosphere, and that constant flow of thoughts, ideas, images and recollections that passes through all our minds – the famous *'stream of consciousness'*. Not everyone cared for this new kind of writing, but it was impossible to ignore. Like James Joyce, Virginia Woolf broke new ground, and not many writers can claim that. The English novel will never be quite the same again.

Chapter Twenty-seven

D H LAWRENCE
1885–1930

The Miner's Boy

David Herbert Lawrence is a writer who was often in trouble and frequently banned. And we all know why, don't we? (Don't worry, we'll get to Lady Chatterley later.) Lawrence was born in Eastwood in Nottinghamshire, one of the five children of a coal miner. His mother, an ex-schoolteacher, was snobbishly convinced she'd married beneath her. (Typical teacher, obviously.) Young Lawrence was intelligent, sensitive and sickly. (Typical writer, really.) He was his mother's favourite and she was fiercely determined her little David wasn't going down the mine. She made sure he did well at school, and at thirteen Lawrence won a scholarship to Nottingham High School.

Work and Study

Urged on by his mum, Lawrence decided to become a teacher. But the training course cost twenty pounds, a small fortune in those days. He left school and briefly got a job in a surgical goods factory to earn the money. (Contrary to certain rumours, he was a sales clerk, not a condom-tester.) He then became an uncertified teacher for four years. When he'd saved up enough, he took up a place on a teacher's training course at Nottingham University. He qualified in 1908, and had a teaching job in Croydon, for the next two years.

A Time of Change

Lawrence was already writing poetry, he'd published a prize-winning short story in the 'Nottingham Post', and his first novel, 'The White Peacock', a Thomas Hardy-type rural romance, came out in 1911. (The boy was clearly going to the bad.) After two years of classrooms in Croydon, Lawrence's health gave way (no wonder!), and he abandoned teaching forever.

Lawrence Takes Off

In 1912 he published his second novel, 'The Trespasser', a tragic tale of a girl obsessed by the memory of her dead violin-teacher, who has committed suicide for love of her. That same year, Lawrence met his

'Is my playing that bad?'

soul mate. Frieda Weekly was the German wife of a university professor. She'd been born Frieda von Richthofen, and was a cousin of Manfred von Richthofen, soon to be famous as a First World War flying ace. Although Frieda was six years older than Lawrence, and married with three children, they fell madly in love and eloped. They stayed together for the rest of Lawrence's life, fiercely devoted and fighting like mad.

Sons and Lovers

In 1913, Lawrence published his first major novel, 'Sons and Lovers', largely a re-telling of his own early life. The ambitious mother, repelled by her coarse coal-miner husband, pins all her hopes on her son. In the process she endangers her son's chances of happiness, since the emotional link between them is unhealthily close. Paul Morel, the hero, falls for spiritual Miriam and the dim but sexy Clara, but neither romance really works. Freed by the death of his mother he decides to go abroad. The book has been called the first really Freudian novel.

Return to England

In 1914 Frieda's divorce came through. She and Lawrence were married. World War One had just broken out, forcing them to return to England. The couple were regarded with deep suspicion by the authorities, who thought they might well be spies. In 1915 Lawrence published 'The Rainbow' a family saga about the Brangwens. It's a powerful study of the loves, marriages and conflicts within one family. It was obviously too powerful for its time – the book was successfully prosecuted for obscenity.

Women In Love

In 1916 Lawrence finished 'Women in Love', which tells the stories of Ursula and Gudrun, who had first appeared in 'The Rainbow'. Ursula loves the sensitive and intelligent Birkin, a school inspector suspiciously like Lawrence himself. Gudrun falls for mine-owner Gerald, whose tough and ruthless front conceals spiritual emptiness. Birkin offers Gerald his friendship and a spot of nude wrestling – which made a memorable scene for Alan Bates and Olly Reed in the later movie. Gerald rejects Birkin's friendship (could he possibly have got the wrong idea?) and goes off to die in the snow, while

Birkin and Ursula find true love. Probably because of the earlier fuss about 'The Rainbow', Lawrence was unable to find a publisher for 'Women in Love'. (The book finally appeared in England in 1921, when it was called 'a study of sexual depravity' and 'an epic of vice.' Today, reviews like that would be worth a fortune.)

Lawrence's Travels

Understandably fed up with the way England had been treating them, Frieda and Lawrence set off on their travels as soon as the war was over. In years to come they lived in Italy, visited Australia, lived for a while in Mexico, went back to Italy, and ended up in southern France. All this time Lawrence, although grappling with ill-health,

was producing novels, poems, and short stories. He wrote 'The Lost Girl', 'Aaron's Rod', a travel book, 'Sea and Sardinia', a novel called 'Kangaroo' (guess where that one was set), and a Mexican novel, 'The

Plumed Serpent'. In Italy, Lawrence turned to painting, and continued to write poetry. True to form, the postal authorities confiscated a volume of his poetry in 1928, and police seized paintings from his London exhibition in 1929. Lawrence wasn't worried. He was hard at work on the best-known, though certainly not the best, of all his books – 'Lady Chatterley's Lover'.

The Lady Chatterley Affair

Beautiful and passionate young Constance Chatterley (steady, chaps, no heavy breathing), is married to wealthy landowner Sir Clifford Chatterley. Sir Clifford is a writer, remote and cynically intellectual. Since he's also crippled by wartime injuries, Connie is starved for love in every sense of the word. She turns to Mellors, her husband's gamekeeper. The two fall madly in love and have a

'I don't understand why so many of you boys want to be gamekeepers?'

passionately physical affair. Lawrence describes their love-making in graphic detail, using well-known four-letter words in the process. Despite its lurid reputation, 'Lady Chatterley's Lover' is a worthwhile attempt to describe physical love in plain and honest language. To be honest, it doesn't really work. Tweeness keeps creeping in. The couple refer to their respective naughty bits as 'John Thomas' and 'Lady Jane' and there's an incident with a daisy-chain you'll never see demonstrated on 'Gardeners' World'.

The book was privately printed in Italy, and for years only well-thumbed smuggled-in copies circulated in England. 'Lady Chatterley's Lover' wasn't published in full in England until 1960 when Penguin Books bravely took the risk of prosecution – and of making a packet – by publishing the uncensored version. The book was duly prosecuted. 'Is it a book,' asked the Prosecutor, 'that you would even wish your wife, or your servants, to read?' The jury laughed, the prosecution failed – and long lines of serious culture seekers formed outside every bookshop. The huntin', shootin' and fishin' magazine, 'Field and Stream' gave the book a serious review. If you didn't mind wading through a good deal of irrelevant material, said the magazine severely, 'Lady Chatterley's Lover' gave a fascinating picture of the work of a gamekeeper on a Midlands estate, with some useful tips on vermin control and the rearing of pheasant chicks . . . Having fired his final shot at the Establishment Lawrence lived for only a few more years. He died in 1930 at Vence in southern France. His body was cremated and the ashes taken to Mexico.

Lawrence and Sex

'Sex,' said Freud, 'is behind everything – and it's catching up all the time!' Lawrence decided sex was important enough to write about seriously. He was a genuine pioneer, and his reputation has suffered ever since. Despite some weird, almost fascist ideas about the deep dark stirrings in the blood, and the need for an intellectual elite, Lawrence at his best is a wonderful writer. The characters he creates, their emotional relationships and the worlds they live in are real and solid, completely convincing.

He was a fine poet too, writing particularly well about natural things:

*'Not every man has gentians in his house
In soft September, in slow sad Michaelmas.'*

And about animals, as in 'Snake':

*'A snake came to my water-trough
On a hot, hot day, and I in pajamas for the heat,
To drink there.'*

Perhaps the obsession with sex is society's problem as much as his. As Lawrence wrote: *'To the Puritan all things are impure . . .'*

Chapter Twenty-eight

J R R TOLKIEN
1892–1973

A Student at War

John Ronald Reue Tolkien, author of the world's most unlikely best-seller, was born in South Africa and brought back to England as a child when his father died. He grew up in Birmingham, attended the King Edward VI School and went on to Merton College, Oxford. At twenty-three, Tolkien went off to war, exchanging the peace of Oxford for the hell of the trenches. Tolkien joined the Lancashire Fusiliers in 1915. A year later he married his sweetheart Edith. They both knew his chances of coming back to her were very small.

A Don's Life

Tolkien served with the Lancashire Fusiliers until the end of the war in 1918. Unlike many others, he survived and came home. He returned to Oxford, taking his Master of Arts degree in 1919. After working on the Oxford English Dictionary, he went on to teach English at Leeds University.

Like any promising young academic, he published a learned work, 'A History of Middle English.' In 1925 he became Professor of Anglo-Saxon at Oxford. And there he stayed for the next twenty years, a highly-respected philologist – philology, as we all know, being the study of ancient languages. He became a typical Oxford don, a pipe-smoking professional academic in a pretty obscure branch of Eng Lit.

Tolkien's Secret

Tolkien loved languages so much that studying existing ones wasn't enough. He just had to invent languages of his own. He created an imaginary world to go with them, called Middle-Earth. Naturally he had to invent a history to go with it, with kings and heroes and monsters and strange creatures. Tolkien had children by now, and he started telling them stories set in his own private world. Some of his Oxford friends encouraged him to try to get one of them published.

A Matter of Hobbit

'The Hobbit' was published in 1937, when Tolkien was forty-five years old. Hobbits are:

> 'little people, about half our height . . . They are inclined to be fat in the stomach; they dress in bright colours (chiefly green and yellow); wear no shoes because their feet grow natural leathery soles and thick warm brown hair like the stuff on their heads (which is curly); have long clever brown fingers, good-natured faces and laugh deep fruity laughs . . .'

'I love your long legs and curly hair.'

A hobbit called Bilbo Baggins is visited by a wizard called Gandalf and a gang of thirteen dwarves. Insisting that he's a skilled burglar, which he isn't, they drag Bilbo off on a dangerous quest to regain the dwarves' stolen treasure from the dragon Smaug. Bilbo survives many terrifying adventures in the course of which he acquires a magic ring. Eventually he triumphs, returning home a hero, and a wealthy hobbit.

'You have some peculiar habits Tolkien.'

'They're Hobbits actually.'

A Small Success

'The Hobbit' was well received, getting good reviews in England, and winning prizes in America. It became a minor classic. Tolkien went on to publish an essay on fairy tales, and two more childrens' stories, 'Leaf by Niggle' and 'Farmer Giles of Ham'. But all the time he was hard at work on another project, one of incredible scope and size, called 'The Lord of the Rings'. Tolkien worked on the new book on and off for the next seventeen years. (The second world war was a bit of an interruption, but he was too old now to have to go off and fight.) By the time the book was finished it was five hundred thousand words long.

'Four hundred and ninety nine thousand nine hundred and ninety six ...'

Tolkien's Epic

'The Lord of the Rings' opens about sixty years after Bilbo's return from his quest. He's about to celebrate his hundred and eleventh – eleventy-first as hobbits say – birthday with a huge party. Then Gandalf reappears. A great war between good and evil is about to begin and Bilbo's magic ring turns out to be of vital importance. It is the One Ring, the Ring of All Power. Unless it is destroyed, by casting it into the volcanic flames of the Mountains of Mordor, in the heart of enemy territory, evil will triumph. Bilbo is too old now for the quest. His nephew Frodo and a group of brave fellow hobbits undertake the task. In the long and dangerous journeys which follow they encounter incredible dangers and all kinds of creatures: enchanters good and bad, men from many different kingdoms, dwarves, savage orcs, trolls, ents (moving, talking trees), subtle, magical elves, and the dreaded Black Riders. Their new friend, the ranger Strider, turns out to be Aragorn, the lost heir to the throne in exile. All ends happily when the ring is destroyed, Sauron the evil enchanter defeated, and Aragorn restored to his throne.

A Slow Start

Because of its amazing length, 'The Lord of the Rings' was published in three volumes. The first, 'The Fellowship of the Ring' and the second 'The Two Towers' were both published in 1954, the third, 'The Return of the King' in 1955. Despite excellent reviews, 'The Lord of the Rings' was by no means an instant success. People just didn't know what to make of it. A short children's book about elves and wizards was one thing – but half a million words in three massive volumes? Who was it *for*? Kids? Adults? Lunatics? Tolkien had written a new kind of book.

'A world full of dragons, Kings and strange creatures — I'm afraid Disneyland's got some tough competition!'

Success at Last

It took several years for 'The Lord of the Rings' to become an established success. The turning point was the publication of lower-priced paperbacks, particularly the big one-volume paperback edition of the entire work. It took off like a rocket, especially in America, where it became a cult. Suddenly 'The Lord of the Rings'

'It's a coffee table version!'

was a best-seller on every campus, and bumper-stickers appeared saying 'Frodo Lives!' Professor Tolkien, who had retired to a country cottage by now, was bemused to find himself a best-selling author and international celebrity. He took it in good part, puffing hobbit-like at his pipe, and enjoying the fame and fortune that had come to him so late in life. He died in peaceful retirement in 1973.

Hobbits Rule OK?

'The Lord of the Rings' was eventually so successful that it virtually re-created the whole genre of heroic fantasy. Today there are whole shelves of Tolkien imitators in every bookshop, yet somehow none of them hold the magic of the original. Partly this is because of the quality of Tolkien's writing, the sheer solid reality of the fantastic landscapes and amazing inhabitants of his magical world. But perhaps the real secret of his success lies not in the extraordinary but in the everyday. It's the hobbits who hold the whole thing together. Small, tubby and timid, caught up in the wars of great men and magical beings, the hobbit makes the most reluctant of heroes. All he asks is to survive and to get home to a blazing fire, a pipe, a flagon of ale and four square meals a day.

Now there's a hero you can really identify with . . .

'For Heaven's sake — I said a flagon!'

Chapter Twenty-nine

WILLIAM HARRISON FAULKNER
1897–1962

The Kid from Oxford

William Faulkner grew up in Oxford – not the university town in England but the country town in Mississippi. He was a simple farmer at heart – and one of the most difficult, subtle and intellectually complex writers in the world. Raised in the racist deep South, he was a liberal who won the Nobel Prize for Literature. He was a quietly-spoken, courteous man, the epitome of Southern charm – and a boozer and brawler of epic proportions.

'Touch of the old Southern charm – eh Mr Faulkner?'

Flying Faulkner

Never a keen student, young Bill Faulkner left school early to work in his grandfather's bank. World War One was under way and Faulkner, raised in the death or glory traditions of the Old South, was keen to get into the action. As soon as he was old enough, he ran off and joined the Royal Canadian Air Force – just too late. The war ended in 1918 when he was still in training as a pilot. Faulkner came home and studied for a while at Mississippi University – he did well in French and Spanish, but got an F for English – and started writing poetry, and odd pieces in college magazines.

New York, New York

He spent some time in New York, where he worked in a bookshop, then came home to Oxford and got a job as postmaster at the University. He used to sit right at the back of the Post Office reading or writing, ignoring customers, and getting extremely grumpy when he had to serve anyone. (Sounds like ideal Post Office material.) Complaints piled up and Faulkner resigned before they could fire

'How can we rob the joint – we can't even get served?'

POST

RING FOR SERVICE

him. He published a couple of volumes of poems, probably written on Post Office time, but they didn't do very well. (Even when he was a world-famous novelist, Faulkner used to say he was really a failed poet.)

Off to Europe

Deciding to see the world, Faulkner took off for New Orleans, hoping to work his passage to Europe. It took him six weeks to find a ship, so he used the time to write his first novel, 'Soldier's Pay', the story of a disabled soldier returning from the war. Then he set off on his trip to Europe, working his passage as a deck-hand. He toured Italy by bike and lived briefly in Paris. (He saw James Joyce in a café, but was too shy to speak to him.)

Home to Yoknapatawpha

On his return to America at the end of 1925, Faulkner found 'Soldier's Pay' had been well reviewed, but wasn't selling. He wrote a second novel, 'Mosquitoes',

satirising the New Orleans artistic colony. That didn't sell either. He wrote a third, 'Flags in the Dust', set in Yoknapatawpha County, a fictional part of Mississippi. It was rejected for publication – but Faulkner had found the theme for his greatest works. His next book, 'The Sound and the Fury', was also set in his invented county. Highly experimental and technically complex, it shows the decline of the once-prosperous Compson family – and, by implication, of the South. The title is taken from Shakespeare's 'Macbeth':

> 'It [life] *is a tale told by an idiot,*
> *Full of sound and fury*
> *Signifying nothing.'*

Much of the story is told by Benjy Compson, the idiot of the quote, who confuses time and place (and the reader) with his disjointed ramblings. Not surprisingly, this didn't sell too well either. Broke

but undaunted, Faulkner took a job as a night-shift coal heaver at the local power station, writing his next masterpiece, 'As I Lay

Dying' in six weeks, between midnight and four a.m. Another Yoknapatawpha County saga, 'As I Lay Dying' was even more complex than the previous book. In fifty-nine, (count 'em), monologues by various characters, it tells of the struggles of the poor-white Bundrens to fulfil the dying wish of their mother, Addie, to be buried in her home town of Jefferson. Most of the book consists of their slow and painful journey with the corpse. It's a powerfully written, deeply-moving book, and – you've guessed it – it didn't sell either.

A Scandalous Success

Faulkner then married his childhood sweetheart, a Southern belle called Estelle, and bought a big house in Oxford, his home town. Obviously, he needed to make some real money. His next novel was a straightforward easy read – bulging at the seams with steamy Southern sex and violence. 'Sanctuary' is a sordid tale of kidnapping, bootlegging, gangsterism, and rape with a corncob. (The gangster is impotent you see – and oh, never mind . . .) Naturally, 'Sanctuary' was an immediate best-seller. Not only that, it convinced Hollywood that Faulkner was just the kind of refined and culturally-minded writer they needed in the movies.

Yoknapatawpha to Hollywood

Over the next twenty years or so, Faulkner raised the wind, when necessary, with occasional script-writing trips to Hollywood. Amongst other films, he worked on the classic Bogart screen versions of Chandler's 'The Big Sleep' and Ernest Hemingway's 'To

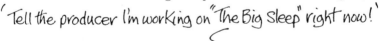
'Tell the producer I'm working on "The Big Sleep" right now!'

Have and Have Not'. But he was really too much of an individualist for the studio system. When it all got on top of him, he used to hit the bottle and vanish for days at a time. Once he asked his producer if he could work at home. The producer agreed, assuming that 'home' meant Faulkner's Hollywood hotel. A few days later, the producer got a postcard – from Oxford, Mississippi, hundreds of miles away.

– and Back Again

Between spells in Hollywood, Faulkner returned, physically and spiritually, to Mississippi and his beloved Yoknapatawpha County. In such complex, densely-packed, interlinked novels as 'Light in August', 'Absalom, Absalom!', 'The Unvanquished', and 'Go Down Moses', he chronicles its tangled and tormented history from early times to the present day. 'The Hamlet', 'The Town', and 'The Mansion', show the rise of the ruthless, amoral Snopes family, whose stealthy rise parallels the decline of old Southern families like the Sutpens and Sartorises. Nor does he avoid the problems of race. Despite their fixed roles in Southern society, his black characters are fully rounded and alive. In 'Intruder in the Dust' Lucas Beauchamp,

an old black farmer, is hated by the redneck whites simply *because* of his quiet dignity and assumption of equality – he doesn't seem to realise that he's black. Because of this prejudice, Lucas is falsely accused of murder, and almost lynched. He's saved by the young white boy who tells the story, and by the boy's lawyer uncle. The South, says Faulkner, must learn to solve its own problems.

Famous Faulkner

William Faulkner's reputation grew slowly but steadily over the years. He lived a quiet country life with his horses and hunting dogs, his pipe and his Bourbon bottle. World fame was thrust upon him in 1950 when he won the Nobel Prize for Literature. 'A Fable', Faulkner's allegorical novel about Christ in the First World War, won the Pulitzer Prize. So too did his last novel, 'The Reivers', set in 1905. Tempted by Boon, a cheerful rogue of a chauffeur and Ned, a racing-mad negro servant, young Lucius Priest, who tells the story, sets off with them on a trip to Memphis – taking, without permission, his stern grandfather's precious new car. Ned swaps the car for a racehorse, and stakes the horse, to be ridden by Lucius, against the car in a coming horse race. If Lucius wins they go home in triumph, with both racehorse and car. If they lose, they're dead . . . Light-hearted, lively and hilarious, 'The Reivers' brings to an unexpectedly cheerful conclusion Faulkner's long series of Yoknapatawpha County novels.

William Faulkner died in 1962, and was buried in the cemetery in Oxford, Mississippi, the town he loved and had lived in for most of his life. As he wrote himself:'I discovered that my own little patch of native soil was worth writing about, and that I would never live long enough to exhaust it. . .'

Chapter Thirty

ERNEST HEMINGWAY
1898–1961

Macho Man

Some male writers feel that they are engaged in a rather sissy occupation. To compensate, they have to be tougher, drunker and generally more macho than anyone else around. Ernest Hemingway is the prime example of this hairy-chested school of scribblers. Big and burly, he boozed, boxed, caught fighting-fish and shot big game. He also wrote some of the finest prose of his time.

'Let me say here and now — I don't think writers are the least bit sissy!'

Hemingway was born in Oak Park, Illinois, son of a doctor and a music teacher. He grew into an extremely large young man, keen on sports and hunting. When he left school, he got a job as a reporter on the 'Kansas City Star'. The First World War was in full swing, and Hemingway was keen to get into the action. Turned down by the Army because of bad eyesight, Ernie enlisted as an ambulance driver in the Red Cross, and was sent to Italy. In 1918 he was at the

Front running a comfort station – not a mobile toilet but a Red Cross post where soldiers were cheered up with chocolate and cigarettes. A mortar bomb exploded right beside him, filling his legs with metal fragments. Despite his own wounds, Hemingway carried a wounded soldier back to safety. When he got out of hospital – where he fell madly in love with a beautiful nurse – the Italians gave him a medal and sent him home.

'You can pin a medal on – but no kissing!'

Hemingway's Paris

Ernie came home to a hero's welcome, and got a job as a reporter on the 'Toronto Star'. In 1921 he married a girl called Hadley Richardson, who had a small income of her own. They set off for Paris, hoping to live on Hadley's money and Hemingway's journalism. Paris in the twenties was *the* place for writers. A favourable exchange rate made a little money go a long way, and Ezra Pound, Gertrude Stein, James Joyce, Scott Fitzgerald and many more writers and artists were living there.

Scott Fitzgerald, who was a bit on the weedy side, tended to hero-worship his burly friend, and often went to him for advice. Fitzgerald was worried about the size of a certain vital piece of his masculine equipment. He felt it didn't measure up to the ones he'd seen on nude statues in the Louvre. After a quick trip to the toilettes, Hemingway was able to reassure him. 'Looking down at it like that, you get a kind of foreshortening effect . . .'

Hemingway also knew James Joyce, and they became great boozing companions. The skinny, short-sighted little Irishman had a habit of picking fights in bars – and then waving forward his giant friend saying grandly, 'Deal with him, Hemingway! Deal with him!'

'The Sun Also Rises'

Hard up but happy, the Hemingways travelled in France and Italy and went to follow the bullfights in Spain. In 1925 Hemingway published a volume of short stories, 'In Our Time', and in 1926 he published his first novel, 'The Sun Also Rises'. It's a romantic tale about the 'lost generation', a rootless group of well-off young Americans looking for a good time abroad. Jake Barnes, the hero, falls for the beautiful and sexy Lady Brett. Jake however lacks a vital piece of equipment – the same one Scott Fitzgerald was so worried about. (It was shot off during the war, presumably by a sniper with a good aim and a nasty sense of humour.) Brett's hardly the girl for a

'Well, look on the bright side – you'll never need a vasectomy!'

platonic friendship and poor old Jake has a miserable time, following her to Spain, where she has an affair with a bullfighter. The book contains some of Hemingway's finest writing, with wonderful descriptions of café life in Paris and bullfighting in Spain, and it got excellent reviews.

'A Farewell to Arms' – and to Wife No. 1

While Hemingway's career was prospering his marriage was on the rocks. In 1926 he fell in love with Pauline Pffeiffer, a young journalist. Hadley and Hemingway were divorced, and he married Pauline in 1927. In the same year he published another book of short stories, 'Men Without Women'.

Hemingway's next novel, 'A Farewell To Arms', was published in 1929. A tragic love story, based on Hemingway's hospital romance in Italy, it got well-deserved rave reviews and excellent sales. The Paris period was over now. Hemingway was over thirty and an established writer. He and Pauline went back to America living in

Key West in Florida, and later in Cuba. He still made frequent trips to Europe, particularly Spain, and for the first time, to Africa. In 1932 he wrote 'Death in the Afternoon', expressing his life-long

fascination with bullfighting. He published 'Winner Take Nothing', a book of short stories, in 1933 and 'The Green Hills of Africa', an account of big game hunting, in 1935.

Back to War

In 1936 the Spanish Civil War began and Hemingway went out as what he called an 'anti-war correspondent'. The experience produced a great book and a new wife. (One of Hemingway's friends said a new wife came with every major work.) The wife was a fellow war correspondent, a tough sophisticated lady called Martha Gelhorn. The book was 'For Whom the Bell Tolls', a story of anti-fascist guerillas in the civil war. The hero, Robert Jordan, has a poignant romance with a refugee girl. (During their night of passion in a sleeping bag *'the earth moves'* – setting a standard difficult for all later lovers to follow.) At the end of the book Robert Jordan stays

behind to cover the guerilla band's retreat, awaiting certain death with heroic calm. (Hemingway once defined courage as grace under pressure.) The book, one of Hemingway's finest, was an enormous success. Like many of his books it was later filmed. The Spanish Civil War was soon followed by World War Two, and it has to be said that Hemingway had a wonderful war. Officially a war correspondent, he carried arms (quite illegally), took part in the fighting, led a band of French guerillas in the liberation of Paris, and personally liberated the bar of the Ritz Hotel.

Post War Blues

Sadly, the war marked the peak of Hemingway's happiness and success. Afterwards it was mostly downhill. His third marriage broke up, and his fourth soon became increasingly unhappy. The high spirits became bullying and bluster, the boozing was turning into serious alcoholism, his health was giving way and he was subject to fits of depression. Hardest of all, his 1950 novel, 'Across the River and Into the Trees', was savaged by the critics. Its hero, the battered old soldier Colonel Cantwell, has a last affair in his beloved Venice with the beautiful young Countess Renata – entertaining her between drinking and love-making with his memories of the war. Everyone had been hoping for the great Hemingway novel of World War Two – and this wasn't it. But the old champ wasn't finished yet. In 1952 he published 'The Old Man and the Sea' a short novel about and old Cuban fisherman, struggling to bring in the biggest fish of his life. Simply and beautifully written, it was a tremendous success, both critically and commercially, and it won the Pulitzer Prize. He made a last trip to Africa and was nearly killed in not one but two plane crashes. In 1954 Hemingway was awarded the Nobel Prize for Literature, though he was too ill to attend the ceremony. His depression worsened and he became suicidal. In 1961 there was an 'accident' with a shotgun. Ernest Hemingway was dead.

'A Moveable Feast'

Hemingway is the victim of his own legend. The boastful macho image concealed a skilled and sensitive craftsman who brought a new strength and simplicity to the business of writing. Just before he died he was working on what was to be one of his finest books. In 'A Moveable Feast', published after his death, Hemingway movingly, and brilliantly, recreates the Paris of the twenties, the days when life was fresh and new, and he was a young writer with everything before him:

'When we came back to Paris it was clear and cold and lovely . . . On the streets the winter light was beautiful. Now you were accustomed to see the bare trees against the sky and you walked on the fresh-washed gravel paths through the Luxembourg Gardens in the clear sharp winds. The trees were sculpture without their leaves when you were reconciled to them and the winter winds blew across the surfaces of the ponds and the fountains blew in the bright light . . . Paris was always worth it and you received return for whatever you brought to it. But this is how Paris was in the early days, when we were poor and very happy.'